COMING IN TO LAND

THE MEMOIRS OF WING COMMANDER BILL MALINS, DFC

COMING IN TO LAND

THE MEMOIRS OF WING COMMANDER BILL MALINS, DFC

EDITED BY CHRIS NEWTON

MEMOIRS

Cirencester

Published by Memoirs

MEMOIRS
AUTOBIOGRAPHIES
& FAMILY HISTORIES

Memoirs Books
25 Market Place, Cirencester, Gloucestershire, GL7 2NX
www.memoirsbooks.co.uk

Copyright ©Malins December 2010

First published in England, December 2010

Edited by Chris Newton
Book jacket design Ray Lipscombe

ISBN 978-0-9565102-3-5

Printed in England

Contents

FOREWORD

In the spring of 1926, as a boy of ten, I suffered the agony of watching my home burn down before my eyes. That was also the year we had to surrender our tenancy of Copthall Farm, Caversfield, to make way for the new RAF station at Bicester, and I remember watching the first aircraft, a Hawker Horsley, arrive at the new airfield and being gripped by conflicting emotions. From that day on I was driven by two very different desires: to see the family farm rise once again from the ashes, and to fly.

The story of my life that follows reflects two contrasting passions; the love of the land and of the farm which has now been in our family for over a century, and the love for flying which I discovered during my wartime career as a pilot in the Royal Air Force. Whether or not I have managed to reconcile these two very different vocations successfully must be for others to judge.

W E V Malins

Hawkwell Farm, October 2010

Introduction and acknowledgments

I would like to thank my family for encouraging me to commit my memories to print, and to record my particular thanks to those who have worked so hard over the past few years to make it possible. My particular thanks to my granddaughter, Victoria Williams, my daughter-in-law, Alison Malins, and to Colin Ford, No.268 Squadron RAF Historian.

In memory of my late wife, Daphne, to whom I owe so much.

Chapter 1

Country boy

I was born at Lords Farm, Bicester, on Sunday September 26th 1915. The old rhyme says Sunday's child is bonny and blithe and good and gay. I hope I have lived up to that over the years since, though my father was away in Germany fighting in the First World War at the time, so things can't have been quite so blithe and gay for him and my mother.

My father was Trooper William Vernon Malins of the Queen's Own Oxfordshire Hussars. He had joined the local yeomanry, and as a farmer he was expected to take his own horse to war with him, which he did. When his regiment, the 2nd Battalion of the Oxford & Buckinghamshire Regiment, went to France in 1914, my father stayed in England on coastal defence. Only when the Battle of the Somme began in July 1916 was he sent to join them.

After peace was declared the regiment went to Bonn as the occupying force, and my father finally returned home in February 1919.

Not Private - Trooper. I was proud of that. A trooper in a cavalry regiment was considered a better man than a private in the infantry. When I went for my interview for a commission in the RAF, it gained me marks.

My earliest recollection of my father must have been the day he returned home from the war. I remember being picked up by a strange man in a rough uniform and being held up to look over the door of the loose box into the pigsty, where a sow was rearing ten little piglets. It was a sandy and black Oxfordshire sow, a very popular breed at that time among the Oxfordshire farmers. The piglets were of course sandy and black as well, and they made quite a picture suckling on their mother.

My father brought his steel helmet back with him from the war. We hung it up in the porch at the front of the farmhouse and for many years we used it as a flower basket, until finally it rusted and could be used no more.

Today Lords Farm is run by my son Tim. It also houses the headquarters of an agricultural equipment manufacturer, but in those days it was just an arable farm with sheep and beef cattle.

My first clear memory of my infant years is of standing at the gate separating the garden of Lords Farm from the front yard and watching the cows with their calves - I wasn't allowed into the yard itself. I found it fascinating to watch the men putting hay and turnips into the two square wooden mangers, and then look on as the animals munched their way through their evening meal.

I wasn't happy just to watch the animals - I wanted to ride them. One day, when I was no more than three or four years old, I climbed on to a cow lying in the yard and it got to its feet with me still clinging to its back. The men were afraid I'd be killed, so they put a fork between its curved horns to hold it down. You rarely see horns on a cow now.

My father had a Suffolk ram which he kept with the flock. He was a friendly old ram with a rounded roman nose and he was very fond of my father, but he didn't like me. He would take a few steps back and then charge and knock me down. One of the farmhands told me that the only way of stopping a ram from knocking you down was to get on to its back and hold on to its fleece. I tried it, and he was right. There's no easier ride than on the back of a woolly lamb or a sheep with its fleece still on, though it helped that I was a bit underweight for my age. It's much more difficult to ride one after early June, when the flock has been sheared.

On hot sunny summer days when the sheep were lying down in the field and sleepily cudding it was difficult to get them to stand up, especially the ram, so I would creep up behind them and leap on to their backs. They would get up and gallop twenty or thirty yards along the field, then stop,

Chapter 1

realise I was still on board and try to throw me off. Generally I would manage to stay on until I'd decided I'd had enough and it was time to leave the poor sheep alone. What fun we had, all those years ago.

I once asked my father what the ram was for. "He's there to keep the fox away" he replied. It was years before I found out the real reason. I wish my father had explained to me then that our 150 ewes were the ram's wives, and that he was the father of all the lambs that gambolled about the fields each spring until they were fat enough to go for slaughter. He could have given me a valuable lesson in the facts of life.

The farmhands used to call me Major Bill, or the Major – it was a name that would stick for the rest of my life, except for my years in the RAF. One day I asked my mother why. She told me that when I was about a year old they had put me on the back of a horse in the yard and one of the farm workers had said "Oh look, it's Major Bill". The Major was a retired Army officer who lived at Slade Farm and he used to ride up Lords Lane on exercise each morning, so I suppose I reminded them of him.

I would ride the horses and ponies as well, at the slightest opportunity. I used to get the ploughman to put me on a horse's back. I would ride it up into the fields and then someone would lift me down so I could run back home up Lords Lane to the farm.

As I grew older I loved working with horses. Ours had to work on a few pounds of oats a day plus hay, but they kept very fit on it. It was a delight for me as a boy to be allowed to take a pair of horses harrowing the fields or behind the drill at planting time, in the spring or the autumn. There was nothing to disturb the peace and quiet of the day. All you could hear was the 'shushing' of the harrow as it pulled through the soil and the birds singing in the hedges and the trees. Today's tractor drivers have to sit in an insulated cab, and all they can hear is the noise of the engine or the pop music on the radio. They don't know what they're missing. It's a terrible shame not to be able to hear the birdsong when you're out working in the fields.

Chapter 1

Haymaking was still done in the old traditional way. The mower was drawn by two horses and it would give you about a four-foot-wide cut. The swathes of cut hay were allowed to dry in the sun for couple of days, after which they would be tedded (turned over to help them to dry) with a horse-drawn tedder and finally put into haycocks, small heaps about two or three feet high and three feet across at the bottom. This allowed the hay to dry out and cure and helped it to shed any rain if there was a shower overnight. The haycocks had to be picked up by hand, but we had a hayloader which picked up loose hay and carried it into the back of a wagon, although it had broken down during the war.

When the hay was dry enough it was "windrowed" with a horse-drawn side rake. This left a continuous line of hay ready to be picked up with the hayloader, which was towed behind. It dropped the hay into the back of the wagon, where one or two men would push it with forks up to the front. In the 1920s the hayloader stayed in the rickyard, gradually getting shabbier, but it wasn't until the late 1930s that it was replaced with a better hayloader which made haymaking a much easier job.

Haymaking was a chancy business, because of the weather. You had to pick the right time or you could waste the whole crop because it got too wet or went past its best.

Harvesting the oats was much easier. It was less at the mercy of the weather than haymaking. The oats had to be left in chocks or stooks and the old saying was that you should let the church bells ring for three Sundays before it was time to carry them and put them into a rick.

I used to enjoy the harvest. Three horses were needed on the binder which cut the corn and bound the sheaves and the leading horse would often want to eat the ears of oats. My grandfather, Grandpa Malins, would get the men to put me on the back of the leading horse, which was always known as the forrester. My job was to hold the right-hand rein tight so that the horse couldn't turn its head to the left and start feeding off the standing crop.

Chapter 1

Building the rick of oats, barley or hay was always fascinating. I enjoyed being allowed to get on to the rick with the two men who were building it as the hay was pitched up to them a forkful at a time by a man standing in the wagon. During harvest he pitched up the sheaves one at a time to a man who placed them carefully around the edge of the rick to make sure it kept its shape and did not bulge to one side or the other. I had a fork with a short handle so I would be less likely to stick it into one of the men working on the rick.

Joe Butler, our carter, was the rick-builder. Joe would throw me into the centre of the rick to keep me from falling off. There was always the danger of being kicked by horses or run over by the iron 'tyre' of a wagon, which could easily break a leg. There had been cases where children had been killed because they got in the way of a wagon.

In September 1920 I started at the Church of England Primary School, on the Bucknell Road in Bicester. I went with my big sisters Marjorie, Joan and Nellie, who were attending the bigger school next to the church. I remember this clearly, because we were joined by Nellie Hayes, who had won a scholarship to the Milham Ford Girls' School in Oxford and was on her way to catch the train into Oxford. Nellie's father lived at Primrose Cottage, halfway between Lords Farm and Bicester.

They were happy years, but there was a terrible sadness just around the corner. In August 1921 I acquired a baby sister, Margaret Nita. One day in June 1923, when she was not yet two years old, Nita was taken ill with appendicitis and had to be rushed into hospital for an operation. At that time we had no car and no telephone, so it was a lengthy business to notify the doctor. Our parents took Nita off to the Radcliffe Infirmary in Oxford, leaving the rest of us at home on our own. It was a hot, sunny day.

We were joined for a lunch of cold chicken by Mary Phipps from the neighbouring farm, who was a friend of Joan's. While we were dismembering the chicken carcass someone said they had the wishbone, so we all said they should make a wish – "but please don't tell us what the wish is, or it won't come true." But we all knew what the wish was - that our baby sister would recover and come safely home from hospital.

Our wish was not granted. Little Nita had contracted peritonitis, and the operation was too late to save her.

Rarely a day has passed in the years since when I haven't remembered Nita. Mother used to bring her to meet me on my way home from school. I would walk up to the bridge with the Lapper children from Gowell Farm, and they would turn left up to their farm while I made my way up Lords Lane on my own. When Nita saw me she would come running to meet me, and I would crouch down so she could fling her arms around my neck and then pick her up and swing her round. Then I'd put her down and she'd say "swing me again", and I'd do it again and again until I was giddy. My last memory of Nita is of her running to meet me in the summer sunshine down Lords Lane. She was a lovely little girl, and it brings tears to my eyes now to think of it. As for my mother, it broke her heart.

In about 1924 my grandfather took me off on my first holiday to the seaside. First we went to London, where we took the underground from Paddington to Kings Cross. Then we took a bus to Finsbury Park and rode on top of a tram through Haringey, Wood Green and Palmers Green to Winchmore Hill, so that my grandfather could point out various important places in North London. I remember him saying "I can remember when all these houses weren't here – when I first came to live in London in about 1874, this was all fields".

Winchmore Hill was where my Aunt Nellie lived. She was married to Griff Berry, the head of the piano manufacturing firm of Nathaniel Berry and Sons, who had a piano factory in Finchley. After a short stay with Aunt Nellie we took the train to Brighton, where my grandmother had taken a house for the summer. For the first time I was able to see the sea and ships and swim in salt water, though I did not really learn to swim until a couple of years later when I stayed with my grandmother at Winchmore Hill and went to the swimming baths at Barrowell Green.

I remember going to Hove with them to see county cricket matches. On Sundays we visited various churches, as my grandfather always attended both morning and evening service in one church or another.

My grandfather had married my grandmother, whose name was Annie Cecilia Madgin, around 1876. He had met her because they attended the same church, St Paul's in Tollington Park, near Finsbury Park. She was the daughter of James Madgin, a builder and developer who had built many houses and a few shops and other business premises on the north side of the Seven Sisters Road. One of the roads they built was Moray Road, and my grandparents moved into one of the houses there shortly after they were married, in about 1877. It was called Moray Road because Mr Macfarlane (my grandmother's sister Harriet's husband), who was in charge of all the joinery in the building firm, came from Morayshire.

My great-grandfather had been a very successful businessman, and when he died he had left an estate of about 200 houses, plus the odd public house and shop, to his two daughters, my grandmother and Harriet. When my grandmother died in 1931 her income from the rents of the properties which had been left to her by her father was about £2100 per year.

In the 1920s and 1930s, holidays were still a luxury. They were few and far between for small farmers like my father. It wasn't until 1928, when he bought a car, that we were able to take a few days off to go to the seaside as a family. By the 1930s we were making day trips to Bournemouth and other places on the south coast, which were only about two hours away from Oxford.

As the 1920s went on it became obvious even to me that farming was becoming less profitable. I remember my father telling my mother over breakfast that the price of corn was falling, and that soon it would be economically impossible to grow corn in England because of all the cheap grain which was being imported from North American and Russia. Around 1922 the wheat price guarantee of £10 a ton which the Government had introduced immediately after the war was discontinued. After that market prices prevailed, and wheat and barley were soon down to about £7 a ton.

Wool was no better. I remember that in 1925 or 1926 the prices were so low that my father didn't sell the wool - he stored it in the granary for a year, only to find that the price had dropped another ha'penny.

Eventually my father realised he would have to start milking to make a living, and in 1926 he began to change the farm from arable to dairy. This must have been a hard decision. In those days it was considered almost undignified for farmers to milk cows – to most of them, farming meant growing arable crops and rearing sheep and beef cattle. The crop consisted of barley, mainly for malting, and kale, swedes and turnips, which were grazed off by sheep in the winter. The sheep provided the fertility to grow the wheat crop. The saying was that the sheep provided the golden hoof.

Milking was the saving grace of many farmers, but it was a dreadful tie to have to milk twice a day seven days a week, unless you had a competent cowman. Many carters and horsemen thought it was beneath their dignity to milk cows. Joe Butler would do most things on the farm, but he would never milk a cow. And of course you had to find the money to buy them, at £25-30 apiece.

After the First World War the Prime Minister, Lloyd George, who led the wartime coalition Government, introduced a scheme to help returning soldiers to start building a living for themselves and their families. The idea was that every man leaving the services should be given the opportunity to acquire five acres of land and a cow. As he grew more successful, he would be able to rent more land from the county council. We saw this working at first hand, because one of the blocks of land bought by the council for this purpose was at Gowell Farm. We had farmed Gowell Farm ourselves until 1918, when we had given it up because my mother found it too much work on top of the other land we rented.

Gowell Farm was divided into three smallholdings. The original small farmhouse and farm buildings, with about 80 acres, were let to a returning soldier called George Lapper, whose children I mentioned above. George became one of the first to start dairying. He was soon milking half a dozen cows and taking the milk round to the doorsteps at threepence a pint, or two shillings a gallon. You could set your clock by George – he would leave for Bicester at five minutes to eight every morning.

The remainder of Gowell Farm, about 80 acres, was divided into two. Alf Richardson took on 30 or 40 acres and a Mr Loveridge-Smith the remainder, which they would work as a smallholding. Both men were returning soldiers and Alf Richardson was also a full time postman, but he had been able to convince the Oxfordshire County Council officer who was in charge of the lettings that he would be able to take on the land while he was working as a postman and if successful, he would then carry on the land as a full-time job and leave his job in the Post Office. Unfortunately neither farm had a water supply, and by 1930, with falling agricultural prices, both fell into disuse.

There were many other small farms with 30 to 80 acres or so which were taken on by returning soldiers who failed to make a success of their opportunities. Others were more fortunate, particularly some of those who took on smallholdings in villages. If the county council decided a few years on that the rent was too low and it was better to realise the property's capital value, the sitting tenant was given the chance to buy the freehold. He might then be able to sell the land and buildings for development, which in some cases might raise as much as a million pounds. The lucky tenant could then use the money to buy a much bigger farm of his own.

Chapter 1

One of my father's first customers was the local workhouse, which was about half a mile away. The workhouse, which had opened in about 1850, housed people who were unable to look after themselves because of poverty or old age. Milk had to be delivered there twice a day, because in warm weather the morning milk would soon go off. My father, or more often Joe Butler, would take the milk to the workhouse in the pony and float and then one of us children would be asked to take the smaller afternoon delivery on a bicycle in time for the inmates' tea at five o'clock.

In addition to looking after the old and poor of the district, the workhouse took in tramps and people on the road looking for work; in the late 1920s and early 1930s there were many of these. The workhouse mistress was a Mrs Parks, whose late husband had been the workhouse master. She had a Mr Hatch and his wife working for her and they would let the tramps and travellers in each day at half past four. The new inmates would have a bath and a meal and set off the next morning after another meal to try the next workhouse.

Mrs Parks lived very comfortably in a flat above the front door of the workhouse. Her prize possession was a circular rose garden, which was tended by the male inmates. There was also a strawberry bed. The Board of Guardians would be invited to tea with Mrs Parks, and in summer they would be served the strawberries from her garden.

The kitchen and dining room of the workhouse were kept immaculately clean and the tables were well scrubbed. Many times I saw the inmates filing in for their tea, which had already been put out on long wooden tables. The men and women went in separately, because their living quarters were separate, even for the married couples.

The women were attired in blue cotton dresses which reached down to their ankles. They were quite shapeless (the dresses, not the women), but they nevertheless served to keep them warm, presumably helped by reasonable underclothes. The men's clothes were provided by Alf Evans, the tailor in Bicester, and they looked very smart in new corduroys, strong boots and Derby tweed jackets and waistcoats. When we delivered milk to the workhouse we would hear their hobnailed boots clattering up and down the corridor.

On a summer Sunday we often saw the men and women from the workhouse out walking along the Bucknell Road. They would look in at Lords Farm and show great interest in the cows and their calves. They seemed as pleased as we were to walk along Lords Lane with its wide, green grass verges and pick the buttercups, dandelions and daisies.

Children of families who were up against it were often sent off with their parents to recover some decency, if that's the right word, in the workhouse. The children would arrive there in rags to come out very respectably dressed, the boys in corduroy trousers and tweed jackets and waistcoats or jerseys and the little girls in frocks which they would wear to go to the primary school or to the church school.

My grandfather served on the board of guardians of the workhouse for many years. He told me he was always asking for a little more money to be spent on better housing, food or bedding to improve the quality of life of these inmates, but he was often overruled, usually, sad to say, by the richer members of the board.

I got to know the inside of a workhouse myself some years later, when I spent ten days in the old workhouse at Newmarket. It had been converted into an emergency hospital, and two days before Christmas 1942 I was taken there with jaundice. It has been my boast ever since that I had once spent Christmas Day in the workhouse, as in the old song: "Twas Christmas day in the workhouse, the coldest day of the year, when in came the workhouse master, his face all flushed with beer. How now you idle paupers, we bring you Christmas cheer....."

I remember a character called Lacey Dick, a powerfully-built man who would come to the farm in the winter to help us with threshing. He got his name because he would buy pieces of leather from the tanneries and cut them into thin strips to make laces, which he would then sell from house to house and farm to farm for a penny a pair.

When I first knew Lacey Dick he was already in his fifties. He and his wife would make benders - a kind of crude tent – by stretching sacks over willow rods. If you had three or four thicknesses of sacks the rain never seemed to get through. The entrance was surrounded by sacking, sloping upwards like a poorly-made Indian wigwam and narrowing at the top to draw the smoke up. They always smelt of smoke just the same.

When you built straw ricks in the those days you put the butts of the sheaves to the outside, and Lacey and his wife used to scratch their backs up against the butts as if they had fleas.

In the summer he and his wife – we didn't know her name, we just called her Mrs Dick - would travel to Essex or Cambridgeshire for the fruit picking, using the workhouses on the way. They would walk ten or fifteen miles a day, so it would probably take them six days or so via Buckingham, Olney and Bedford. There were workhouses at Bicester, Woodstock, Chipping Norton, and west into the Cotswolds, Shipston-on-Stour and all the way to the Welsh Borders.

Men hated the thought of ending up in the workhouse - they would go on working as long as they could rather than end up there. But when we didn't see Lacey Dick and his wife any more, we thought that's where they must have ended up.

When they pulled the workhouses down they found lots of sixpenny pieces stuck in the walls. People had put them in there for safe keeping because they knew that any money they had would be taken from them.

There were laws restricting child labour even back then, but the farmers didn't seem to take much notice of them. In the school records at Islip from the 1880s the headmaster had made notes about the number of children absent at harvest time, blaming the farmers for keeping them away from school. People used their children for gleaning – picking up left-over ears of corn. After the last sheaf was taken out of the field, anyone could go in and pick up the scattered ears of corn that were left. I can remember gleaning in Gilbey's field, opposite Lords Farm, after the First World War, when I was four or five. Women with skirts down to their ankles would be picking up the heads of corn and putting them in their aprons. If they worked hard enough they could get enough corn to feed five or six chickens for the rest of the winter. That was how we lived in those days.

One of the joys of harvesting was hunting rabbits. As we got towards the middle of the field the rabbits would be confined to an ever-decreasing area in the middle. Over the last half an hour they would start to run out and seek refuge in the hedges. They had to jump over or swerve round the sheaves lying on the ground which had not yet been picked up.

When they started to break cover, the men would be waiting for them armed with heavy sticks. You could often kill a rabbit before it reached the safety of the hedgerow.

My father and his friends had guns. They would stand in a safe position on the edge of the crop, where they could get an easy shot at a bolting rabbit.

Threshing was another interesting time. We had to lay on additional help, which was easy back then because there were always unemployed men who would enjoy a day's threshing and the pay that went with it. We had to order the threshing box and coal for the steam engine that drove it. We needed enough coal for two or three days' threshing and you were expected to fill up the coal box on the steam engine to the level it had been when it arrived. The man in charge of the threshing tackle had to come half an hour earlier than anyone else to start the fire box to get the steam up, and it was considered a matter of pride to have the engine running dead on seven o'clock.

There were often a few rats at the bottoms of the ricks, and we all did our best to ensure they didn't get out to survive another day.

By 1925 my father was milking more cows, so we began looking for another outlet for our milk. We found one almost on our doorstep when we were approached by one of the staff from Sir Lindsay Parkinson & Co, who were building all the hangars and other buildings for the new Bicester airfield, including the airmen's mess, the sergeants' mess, the officers' mess, complete with squash court, and all the married quarters for the officers and other ranks. They wanted milk delivered twice a day to the workmen's canteen.

By the late summer of 1926 much of the building work at the airfield was completed and we started delivering milk night and morning to the new married quarters as well. When we lost the contract for supplying milk to the workhouse later that year it didn't matter too much, as we were selling more and more milk to the airfield.

As the 1920s progressed our dairy herd was increased to seven or eight cows or more and we were getting threepence a pint, or two shillings a gallon. Dairy farmers who sent their milk by train to Express Dairies or United Dairies in London were getting only tenpence a gallon, less than half as much.

Soon the dairy companies started collecting the milk in lorries, which made the job easier. They set up dairies dotted around the country to serve as collection centres. That way the milk was refrigerated and got to the dairies more quickly, so it became a better, safer and cleaner product.

In addition to Lords Farm and Gowell Farm we worked Copthall Farm at Caversfield. Copthall Farm did not have a house, but there were buildings in which we could winter cattle.

Gowell Farm had a small cottage where one of the foremen lived. Our employees in the early 1920s had been reduced to three men – Joe Butler, Harry Cripps and little Georgie, whose surname I never knew. Joe Butler was a very handy man to have on the farm. You could rely on him to keep a mowing machine and a binder running. In the winter he would make hurdles by cutting branches from the willow trees along our brook in the Little Slade, one of our fields.

Joe lived in Tintown, a row of tiny cottages in the Banbury Road, Bicester. He and his wife shared a little cottage with a corrugated iron roof and a dirt floor. To supplement their pay they did our laundry, including the hard 'flyaway' collars my father wore, with the tie on the outside of the collar. They were already very old-fashioned by the 1920s.

In Bicester there was a rather run-down area called Crockwell, where beds were available in lodging houses at a shilling a day and men could have the use of a fire for cooking breakfast and an evening meal. That was where Harry Cripps lived. The lodging houses were owned by Mr Palmer, the rag-and-bone man, who paid us fourpence each for rabbit skins.

Men like Harry found the lodging houses a convenient way of living. On a winter's evening as you cycled through Crockwell you would often catch the smell of herrings being fried on a fire in the lodging house. Herrings at that time cost about a penny each. Breakfast would probably have been tea and bread and butter. For the midday meal most men would have a chunk of bacon with the top off a cottage loaf and some cheese and onion - the onion disguises the fat bacon. I grew up enjoying crusty bread with cheese and an onion, which I used to take out and eat with the men in the cart hovel when they stopped for dinner.

In the 1920s all the day-to-day work on the farm was still done by hand. We had no machinery of any sort. Various devices were used to lighten the load, such as a yoke which fitted across the shoulders and had a chain each side to carry buckets of milk from the cow shed to the dairy, where it was cooled before putting into the churns.

Farm transport was all horse-drawn, a trolley or a wagon or for local journeys to the town a pony and trap, known as a buggy. We also had a milk float which would also carry half a dozen sheep, which was useful if you needed to go into town to the local corn merchant to buy seeds or other supplies for the farm. It would take about half a ton quite comfortably. We had a reliable pony that would make the journey from Bicester to Lords Farm in about ten minutes.

Some farm workers at that time kept a pig in the cottage garden. They would kill at least one pig a year, which would keep them in bacon and ham for a few months. Those with larger families might kill two in a year. Some of these farm workers had big leaded trays in which they could cure the bacon sides. We had three of these at Lords Farm, but they were lost in our fire in 1926.

Country life was so simple, and it was all great fun for a young lad growing up like me.

Chapter 2

Fire at Lords Farm
1926-27

In 1926 we had a very dry start to the spring, with no rain for two or three weeks. The thatched roofs on the cowshed and stable and the long barn adjoining the roads were all bone dry, and a strong easterly wind was blowing.

On the morning of Monday March 22 I was with my mother, helping her to feed our day-old chicks in the shed at the back of the farm. Foden steam wagons - small road trains used to carry roadstone – used to pass the farm and stop at the culvert on Lords Lane to take on water for steam. It seems a spark from one of these wagons settled on the thatch, and within seconds, fanned by the strong wind, flames sprang up on the thatch.

At about nine o'clock one of the workmen saw smoke rising from the cowshed and shouted to my father. They put up a ladder and started drawing buckets of water from the pump and throwing it on to the thatch. But the wind was too strong. The fire spread to the top of the roof and down the other side. The wind blew the sparks across the yard, and within minutes the fire had spread to the thatch on the long barn, next to the house.

The farmhouse had a slate roof, but that didn't save it because it was linked to the barn by wooden beams. The beams caught fire and carried the fire into the roof of the farmhouse. The ancient timbers in the roof quickly caught fire and the farmhouse, which had three storeys, began to burn from the top.

Father quickly realised that the fire was out of control. He rushed over and told me to ride into Bicester and report the fire to the first policeman

Chapter 2

I saw, then go on to the fire station and tell the man in charge of the fire brigade, who was the Bicester surveyor, a Mr Smith.

I rode there on my bike as fast as I could. I stopped to tell a policeman who was standing outside the Midland Bank what had happened, but he didn't seem very interested. He told me to go to the fire station, but when I got there Mr Smith said that the horses needed to draw the fire engine were away harrowing a field down the Launton Road.

I dashed off to find the field and the horses, which were being worked by a man called Tommy Pilbeam. I ran up to Tommy and told him he had to take his horses to the fire station as fast as he could go.

"Oh dear" said Tommy. "One of the 'orses has cast a shoe. He's going to have to be shod 'afore he goes on the road to pull that fire engine."

Waiting for the blacksmith to shoe a horse while our house burned down did not seem such a good idea, so I persuaded Tommy Pilbeam to take the horses to the fire station as they were, and they were duly harnessed to the fire engine. In the meantime Mr Smith had collected three or four council workers who were also part-time firemen, and they all set off at a gallop for Lords Farm, with me following on my bicycle.

When we reached the farm, all the thatched buildings were ablaze and the roof of the farmhouse was burning fiercely. The pump on the fire engine was driven by steam, so the firemen had to light a fire on the engine and wait for it to heat up before they could pump water. The firemen took their hose to the pumping station on Howes Lane, about 200 yards from the farm. Unfortunately the pipes had been flushed over the weekend, so there was very little water left in the water tower. The firemen had to take their hoses on down to the stream which ran under the road about a hundred yards from the farm. This meant that the water had to be pumped uphill, and some of the hoses burst under the pressure.

The horse-drawn fire engine only attended one more fire after that, at Weston-on-the-Green. When it was going round a corner, the horses were being driven too fast and one went down on its knees, which were badly grazed, but it carried on galloping to Weston. A few weeks later a new fire engine, built by Merryweathers of London, was delivered to Bicester. Both cart and pump were driven by a petrol engine.

By the time the firemen had finally got their hoses to play on to the farmhouse, it was ablaze from top to bottom and the cowshed, stable and barn were nearly burned out.

Unfortunately one of the horses which my father had turned out into the yard slipped back into the blazing stable, unnoticed by any of the men through the smoke. She was our best mare, a very docile creature - the men used to let me ride her when they were going to a field to plough. The burning roof collapsed on the poor horse and she was engulfed by the flames.

I was at the back of the house, sitting with my mother in an open shed. She was shocked and quite distraught. While I was talking to her I saw one of her dogs, Boxer, run into our back kitchen, where it used to spend the night. As it went in through the door a big shower of sparks went up - the roof had collapsed on to the dog. Boxer too was burned to death.

That dog was a great favourite of mine, so I was greatly saddened. I had lost two of my greatest animal friends at once.

My sister Marjorie had celebrated her 21st birthday on March 4, and most of her presents were lost in the fire.

The fire soon burned itself out after that, but by mid-afternoon the buildings were smoking ruins. We had nowhere to sleep that night, so Marjorie stayed with my maternal grandmother, Grandma Steele, in Islip, and Nellie and Joan went to my father's parents in London Road, Bicester. Mr and Mrs Phipps at Caversfield kindly offered us a room for the night, and the next day I was told to cycle to Islip to stay with Grandma Steele and Marjorie. My grandma had a four-bedroomed house called Fairlight, so there was plenty of room there, and I stayed on there for three months and went to Dr South's school in the village. It was a very good school - better in fact than the one I had been attending in Bicester.

My grandmother at Islip had been widowed in 1915 when my grandfather died of a heart attack and she lived with her youngest son, my uncle Alfred, who was working with Arthur Malins, my father's first cousin, in his engineering business in Little Clarendon Street in Oxford.

Around this time I had an outbreak of ringworm and boils on the back of my neck, which forced me to take several weeks off school. My grandmother began to treat them every couple of hours with hot fermentations, pink lint dipped in boiling water and applied to the skin, and they improved rapidly, possibly because we were now using mains water, which was probably a good deal purer than the water from the pump at Lords Farm. After three or four weeks I was considered fit enough to go back to school at Islip, but I had missed the eleven-plus exam (then known as the Scholarship).

I quickly made friends with the boys at Islip school, particularly Gordon Sherrell, the son of the Station Master. Gordon and I used to wander up the railway line from Islip station and I recall finding delicious wild strawberries growing in the cutting.

The teaching seemed much better at Islip. My mother's cousin Beatrice Steele was the second teacher, under the headmaster, Mr Stanway, who was a very likeable and fair headmaster who offered me lots of help and instruction. I found the other teachers kinder, more attentive and more helpful as well.

It was at Islip that I had my first introduction to Shakespeare, as the class into which I was put, aged ten, was doing King John. The first lines I ever heard in Shakespeare were these:

> *Heat me these irons hot; and look thou stand*
> *Within the arras: when I strike my foot*
> *Upon the bosom of the ground, rush forth,*
> *And bind the boy which you shall find with me*
> *Fast to the chair: be heedful: hence, and watch.*

Chapter 2

I would enjoy fishing in the Cherwell with my Uncle Alfred, who was an expert angler. We caught perch or roach, and most of the villagers had their own recipes for cooking them. When my grandmother fried them, however, I found they didn't compare with sea fish.

During the Easter holiday before I started at Islip School I enjoyed accompanying my Uncle Ted, Edward Steele, who was still running the family building business. This was largely dependent on the church commissioners, who owned almost all the property in Islip, including most of the farms. Fortunately they had almost continuous work to offer him and his staff of about four men. He was also the funeral director for practically the whole of Islip and the seven Otmoor towns.

I remember Uncle Ted repainting the sign for the Nut Tree at Murcott, and helping him to put in a large coal-burning kitchen range in a farm. He was also responsible for looking after the newly-installed electrical generator and storage plant at Woodeaton Manor.

My eldest sister Marjorie continued to work in Oxford, first with a dressmaker and later as a buyer at Webbers, the department store. My second sister Joan would be going to the grammar school, while my other sister Nellie continued at the Church of England school in Bicester.

I remember that on summer afternoons in the holidays I used to milk one of our more docile cows. Chetwode was her name, after the estate where we'd bought her. We had to drive her, with two or three other cattle my father had bought, about nine miles. That might sound a long way, but such a journey was quite normal in those days. There was very little traffic on the road. There would be one man in front to close any open gates and stop any gaps the cattle might get through to trespass on to other farmers' fields. He would stay blocking the gap until the cattle had passed by, then get back on his bicycle and overtake them and do it all again until they reached their destination.

I would milk Chetwode every afternoon at a quarter to four and take the milk, which was only two or three pints, to the workmen's canteen on

Skimmingdish Lane. I found this no hardship, particularly as my father would give me fourpence to go to the cinema. I was very grateful for that, as the cinema, which occupied the old corn exchange behind the Crown Hotel in Bicester, was the only real entertainment in Bicester.

When I wasn't milking I would help the bricklayers who were rebuilding Lords Farm after the fire. My main job was to clean the old bricks by knocking off the mortar with a small butcher's cleaver. I was allowed to climb up the ladder and work alongside the bricklayer and the labourer who supplied him with bricks and mortar. There was no rail to stop me falling over the side, but the men were always very careful to make sure I was kept well to the inside of the planks.

By November 1926 two downstairs rooms at Lords Farm had been completed, which meant that my mother and father and I could now move into the old kitchen and part of the old dining room, which had now been partially repaired.

My grandfather was deeply affected to see the farm he had bought as a young man burned to the ground. 1926 was the year of the General Strike, and I overheard him talking to the builder, Jonas Harris, who told him that the timbers for the flooring and the roof were being delayed because of it.

I remember hearing him express his sympathy for the miners. "They can't press the miners any more, they can't expect them to work any harder and take less money" he said. "If they go on like this, there'll be a minor revolution." I never expected my grandfather to speak like this, as he was a dyed-in-the-wool Conservative. Nevertheless, he was well aware that the working classes were being ground down to breaking point.

My grandfather didn't live to see the revolution he predicted, but in 1931 there was a mutiny at Cromarty Firth at Invergordon in Scotland, when the Navy refused to sail. This was a result of the cuts imposed by the National Government after the Labour Government elected in 1929 had been dissolved. The naval ratings' marriage allowances had been cut to the point where they could barely survive.

My grandfather, who had gone to work in the legal department of Islington Borough Council, had been engaged in administrating the Poor Law for the Borough and he had seen the abject poverty in Islington at that time. Although he remained a staunch Conservative, he always had the interests of the working class at heart. I too saw some of the poverty in Islington, as one of the roads in the area which had been developed by my grandmother's father – Campbell Road in Finsbury Park - was a relic of early Victorian times. The housing there was disgraceful. On hot summer days when I stayed with them in London and went to visit a relative in Durham Road, I would see the women and children sitting on their doorsteps in the sun. Campbell Road was finally demolished at the end of the war, and they never rebuilt it.

While I had been away from Lords Farm a small wooden building had been constructed in the orchard to accommodate my father and mother. I joined them there in June or July 1926. Living in that little hut was not the hardship you might imagine. It was a well-constructed wooden building which had a coal-fired stove and an oil stove with four burners and the equivalent of four hot plates. The door of the hut faced south-east, so we had the sun shining into the doorway all through the morning and up to about three o'clock. It was delightful to have breakfast outside on a little table with the morning sun shining on my Shredded Wheat and eggs and bacon before I went off to school. Those months must have been difficult for my mother, but I never once heard her complain.

In the November we were finally able to move back into the farmhouse, where at first we lived in a single room - the old kitchen, rebuilt at almost twice its previous size. Finally the rebuilding work was completed and we were able to take over the new bedrooms. My sisters then joined us. In March 1927, a year after the fire, the family was once again reunited.

The little hut which had served us so well since the fire wasn't wasted, as Harry Jennings, one of our workmen, and wife moved into it. They stayed there until Harry left us some years later.

Once we were back at Lords Farm I joined my sister Nellie at the Church of England School in Bicester, which I didn't like very much. I thought the teaching was not nearly as good as it had been at Dr South's School at Islip, and my last 18 months there were not a very happy time.

From there I went on to Bicester Church of England Secondary School, which became a secondary modern school. The girls and boys were separated in those days and we had a girls' playground and a boys' playground. I remember my mother giving Nellie a flask of cocoa, and Nellie refusing to let me come into the porch to drink it. She would pour it into the top of the screw top and make me stand outside in the snow and drink it there.

Things were better at home. Our new farmhouse was a very much improved and more comfortable house than it had been before the fire. The old building which we had called the back kitchen now housed a second cooking range and became an integral part of the farmhouse. Before, you had to go out of the back door, walk two paces and turn right into the back kitchen. Now it was all part of an extended back kitchen which included a new flight of stairs to take us up to our bedrooms.

There was a scullery, a spacious new larder and, a few paces outside the back door, a dairy which we could use for milk storage. Here we kept the leads, big zinc-covered three-foot square containers where we cured the hams and bacon from our home-killed pigs.

Another compensation for the fire was the arrival of a mains water supply. My grandfather had laid water on in about 1910 as far as the field next to the farm, but he had never taken it all the way to the farmhouse because he thought the pump by the front door of the farm was adequate.

Later that year a hot-water system was installed to serve the downstairs kitchen and scullery and the bathroom, which had not yet been completed.

Chapter 2

So now we had a farmhouse which was vastly more convenient, with more storage space and more room for people using the kitchen, pantries and larder and storage facilities.

All we needed now was electricity, but for some reason my father never got round to making the small investment needed to have electricity connected from the mains supply lines, which were only 200 yards away. We would have to wait the best part of 20 years for that.

When we moved back in, the front garden, which had mainly been used for vegetables, was little more than a mass of debris thrown out during the fire and in clearing the house before rebuilding started. My mother asked Harry Jennings and another of our employees, Alf Bannister, to restore it. There was plenty of room in the main part of the garden on the south side of the house to grow vegetables. We also had apple trees there, two of which were about a hundred years old but still yielding a good annual harvest.

The front garden held an old pond which had provided drinking water for overwintering cattle. Jennings and Bannister carried soil from the fields to fill the pond in, and dug a ditch so that surplus water could be drained away from the garden. They made an excellent job of it. They also put in a circular path in the largest part of the garden, and later that summer we bought some rose briars from a local man who made pocket money from digging up briars from the hedgerow and selling them to local people, who then budded them with buds from their rose trees.

While we were living in the little hut my mother had had great help from a Mrs Wall from the Slade Farm cottages. She was the daughter of the stud groom for Oliver Gilbey, a rich wine merchant who had bought the farm opposite ours. Doris Wall was an expert gardener, and she taught me how to bud our roses. They were a dark red variety, and we christened them Doris Palmer, after Doris' maiden name. They lasted many years.

By 1930, thanks to a great deal of hard work, the garden was so delightful that my mother invited a photographer, Harris Morgan, to come and take some photographs of the garden with her standing in the middle of it.

Apart from the flowers, one of her greatest pleasures was to dig the first new potatoes. She would often get me to accompany her into the garden just to lift some of the soil and feel whether the potatoes were big enough to dig. If one looked large enough then a couple of roots would be dug up, and from then on we would have new potatoes for lunch whenever we wanted.

The large lilac tree which is now in the front garden of Orpington, the bungalow we built for my aunt next to Lords Farm, was grown by my mother, who cut a slip from one of the lilacs in the old garden – she simply put it into the ground and left it to grow.

On the walls around the front garden was a splendid display of the plant Sempervivum crassulacae, better known as the house leek. My mother said it had been there since before she came in 1904. Over the years sections of the wall would repeatedly collapse, but each time they managed to retrieve some of the plants from the debris and replant them into the newly-built wall. Our house leek required very little care. It was a lime-loving plant, so it flourished on the limestone walls and on the mortar, which was a mixture of three parts soil to one part lime, which had been commonly used for building in the early 1800s.

The old garden also had an ancient pear tree. It produced a lot of fruit, but the pears were extremely hard and were only worth cooking after they had been allowed to ripen in the sun. They then had to be peeled, cored and stewed before you could eat them. We also had a prolific Victoria plum tree.

We had only one eating apple tree, which produced rosy apples of excellent quality. We never knew what variety it was, but we thought it could have been in the garden since the mid 1800s.

At Gowell Farm there were damsons growing wild. Although we gave up the tenancy there in the early 1920s I can just recall going there with my mother to pick damsons out of the hedgerows. It was quite normal a couple of hundred years ago to grow fruit in hedgerows. Today our farm at Souldern, Wharf Farm, has many plum trees. Two railway lines run through part of the farm and we believe the plums are the result of railway workers throwing plums out of their hut nearby, many years ago.

In the early autumn we would pick wild blackberries from the hedges, and sometimes we found field mushrooms. There was always the wildlife, particularly rabbits, which were considered quite a delicacy in the 1920s. We particularly enjoyed rabbit pie with crab apple jelly. My mother was an excellent cook, and later so was my wife. A couple of decades later of course rabbits disappeared from the table in England because of the arrival in the 1950s of that hideous disease myxomatosis. In France rabbit is still more expensive than chicken, and I can understand that as I prefer rabbit to chicken any day.

Today, the best part of a century later, 14 or 15 of us sometimes sit down to a family Sunday lunch together. On these occasions everything on the table has been produced on the farm, from the meat course to the fruit and fresh cream.

The glorious summer of 1927 came to an abrupt end in the September, with heavy rain. The pathway from the hut to the house and barn, which was nearing completion, was deep in mud. Probably as a result of the cold and wet I contracted pleurisy, and had to be moved into the partially-completed dining room. I spent about ten days recovering, attended by Dr Long.

Both Grandpa Malins and my father were very experienced horsemen. My great-grandfather had been a horse dealer, among his many activities, none of which had been very successful. He had however reared and broken some magnificent ponies and my father had learned a lot more about horsemanship when he joined the Oxfordshire Yeomanry.

When my grandfather had married his rich heiress and moved into Moray Road in London in about 1877, he had sometimes bought London bus horses that had 'gone off their feet' – that is, the hard London streets had made their feet too sensitive for work on the road, but they could still be usefully employed on farms. Occasionally my father had to ride these horses from north London to Bicester. The journey normally took two days, so he would break the journey overnight at a coaching inn in Watford.

My father's cousin Jack Malins, who was born in Islip and farmed at Weston-on-the-Green, told me just before he died that when he was a lad of ten my grandfather had got him to ride a horse back to Finsbury Park while my grandfather drove a four-wheel carriage that he'd had specially built for him by a coachbuilder in Holloway. It might be described as a poor man's Phaeton. Jack told me that he had ridden a light-legged horse, complete with saddle, all the way to London, but my grandfather changed horses when they reached the Holloway Road and Jack was told to drive the pony and the four-wheel carriage while my grandfather rode the pony down into Finsbury Park.

The four-wheel carriage was an elegantly-built vehicle which carried four people. My grandfather used to delight on summer evenings in taking my grandmother for a drive, usually to Stratton Audley via Poundon crossroads and then through Stratton Audley Park to Fringford and back to Lords Farm. When we dropped my grandmother back at the house in Bicester and the carriage was parked in the coach house behind the house, I had the job of taking the pony back to Lords Farm, unharnessing it and putting it into the field. I loved doing this because it meant I could ride back through Bicester at seven or eight o' clock on a summer's evening.

The longest trip I ever did with my grandfather was just before the fire, so it must have been in 1925. He had to go on council business to Murcott, Fencott, Islip and Oddington. It was a cold November day, and it must have been a Saturday or I wouldn't have been off school. We called at various houses and then stopped at the Nut Tree in Murcott, where he had a glass of beer and I had a lemonade and a packet of crisps. When we got to Islip we lit the candles in the carriage lamps and I clearly remember going along the old road at Wendlebury and seeing the moon reflected in the little stream that runs beside the road along to Promised Land Farm. We would have got back to Lords Farm at about half past six. I wasn't cold because we would have two large rugs which we laid over our knees, and I could pull my rug up to my chest. But it was unusual for a small boy to spend the best part of a long day in a pony and trap.

In December 1927, Grandpa Malins died. This was a terrible blow, as he had meant more to me than my father. He was very much kinder to me than my father ever was, and always helped me in my school work. His death certainly ruined that Christmas. All in all the 1920s were not a happy decade for us, with the loss of little Nita, the death of my grandfather and that dreadful fire.

In his drawing room at home my grandfather had a revolving bookcase which contained 24 volumes of the Encyclopaedia Britannica, published in the 1880s or 1890s. The bookcase had been specially made by a carpenter to accommodate the encyclopaedia. If there was anything my grandfather wanted to know he would take me into the drawing room and pull round the part of it which formed a desk, then revolve the bookcase until the correct volume came round so that he could remove it and put it on a special sloping shelf built into the bookcase. Then he'd thumb through it until he found the answer I was looking for.

My grandfather had an interest in practically everything. On clear frosty nights, before he got on his bicycle to cycle back to Bicester, he would point out to me the various stars, starting with the Pole Star and the Plough. I've forgotten most of them since, but he was a most helpful old gentleman and very kind to me.

He had been a good cricketer and he enjoyed throwing a cricket ball for me to catch. I still have the ball he won bowling for his club in north London in 1884. It is embossed in gold leaf to the effect that Mr W. Malins was awarded this ball for the best average bowling, 1884.

My grandfather had encouraged my sister Nellie and me to be runners. He would tell us both to run around Home Ground, next to Lords Farm, then give a penny or tuppence to the winner. He would let my sister have a few yards start, so it was difficult for me to catch her. He would join us in the fields to play rounders and take his turn as if he was a child.

My Aunt Dora had been looking after my grandmother, along with a full-time nurse who was the mother-in-law of Jack Taylor, the butcher from The Causeway in Bicester. Dora and her husband Ted Prince had not enjoyed living in Bicester, and after my grandfather's death they all moved to London. They bought a house at 4 Orpington Road, Winchmore Hill, about a hundred yards from my grandmother's sister Harriet at 3 Station Road.

This meant my father had to have a car to visit my grandmother. He bought a second-hand Morris Cowley saloon, which cost about £120 – they were £160 new. It had been a demonstration example from the Morris Garages in Oxford, and its registration number was WL 7110. It served us very well for many years.

When I returned to Lords Farm from Winchmore Hill at the end of my 1928 summer holiday (I had stayed with my grandmother while taking part in the Elementary Schools All England Athletics Championships) it was back to work to help on the farm. By now I was getting bigger, fitter and stronger and I could do rather more work. My pony Tommy had died through old age, but we had a new pony, Flossie, who was very fast. She was a good pony to use for the float, which we used to transport hurdles and sheep equipment on the ploughing in winter. The wheels of the float dug into the ground and it was hard work for the pony to pull it.

By now Harry Cripps had left us, as had little Georgie, but Harry Jennings had proved an excellent cowman and a quick milker. In fact Harry was a jack-of-all-trades, and master of most of them. He would deliver the milk to the aerodrome after milking in the morning and again in the evening. Later we bought a little Morris Eight van, which allowed us to deliver a churn of milk to the airmen's mess and to the officer's mess more easily than on a bicycle.

As a young lad Harry had been a skilled poacher, and I learned a lot of fieldcraft from him. He was deadly with a shotgun and he also had a powerful BSA air rifle, which he used to shoot rabbits or pigeons, for which my mother was always grateful.

I shot my first rabbit when I was 14 and I proudly took it home. Fortunately it was a three-parts-grown one and not one of the old does enkindled with three or four youngsters. My mother was absolutely delighted with it - she was an absolute master of rabbit pie. From then on I was not only allowed out with the twelve-bore, I was actively encouraged.

I shot pigeons too. They were a menace in those days – they still are - and they congregated in scores, sometimes hundreds, to feast on our new green crops during the winter months. But they too were a wonderful example of country food, and my mother knew how to make a brace of pigeons taste like partridges. Eighty years on, I can still taste them.

Chapter 3

Schooldays and sporting success
1928-1938

In the summer of 1928, when I was at Bicester C of E Secondary School, I was selected to represent Oxfordshire in the National Schools Sports, the finals of which were held at Stamford Bridge, Chelsea Football Ground. I was the reserve in the under-14 100 yards and 220 yards races. My mother and my uncle Ted came to watch, and afterwards they took me back to the house where Dora, Ted and my grandmother lived in Winchmore Hill.

Sometimes my Great Aunt Harriet would come to tea and we'd go shopping on Broadway. Harriet was a beautiful woman in her seventies - she lived to be two months short of her 100th birthday. I remember her telling me how surprised she was that Ted had not returned to work during the war when other men of his ability had done so. He had been a book-keeper with Dobreze and Co, which was a big shipping agent - they shipped meat into England from Australia. They went bankrupt in 1925, at the start of the depression, so he was living in Bicester when the fire broke out in 1926.

It was Ted who built most of that wooden house. Aunt Dora didn't want him to go back to work because he was so useful in the house with her stroke-ridden mother, even though she had a full-time nurse.

One day I sat out on the lawn in the sunshine to talk to my grandmother. She told me that she had always promised my grandfather that she would send me to the county school at Bicester (which became the grammar school), and it was now time to honour that promise. I was absolutely delighted, as my sister Joan was already there – she left the year I joined. I had friends who had been to small, lesser-known public schools and I had always dreamed that one day I would be able to attend such a school. So I never returned to my Bicester school.

I had learned that famous poem by Sir Henry Newbolt that goes:

There's a breathless hush in the close tonight
Ten to make and the match to win,
A bumping pitch and a blinding light
An hour to play and the last man in.
And it's not for the sake of a ribboned coat.
Or the selfish hope of a season's fame,
But his Captain's hand on his shoulder smote,
"Play up! Play up! And play the game!"

I thought what a wonderful thing it must be to go to a school where you could learn Shakespeare and play cricket on a field in front of the school. The local grammar school was not exactly a public school, but it would do very well for me.

The county schools had been introduced to provide a secondary school education beyond the school-leaving age, which was then 14. There weren't enough pupils of scholarship standard to fill these schools, so about two thirds of the pupils were fee-paying. The average age in my first year was about 12 and I was always up in the top two or three positions in the class, although I'd never taken the scholarship. A lot of those who paid fees would be at the bottom of the class academically - they were only at the school because their parents could afford it.

The scholarship children had bright new blazers, because they were given a clothing allowance. If you were bright enough but still hadn't got money, you had to buy indoor shoes. I noticed that the boys from Kidlington and Kirtlington who'd won scholarships had nice thick crepe-soled brown shoes to wear that they kept in their lockers. In fact most of them dropped out at 15 because, bright as they were, their fathers thought they ought to be back earning a living.

I started at the school in September 1928 and quickly made friends with several boys, mostly local farmers' sons. I made a very great friend in a boy called Cyril Nash, from the village of Bucknell, who remained a friend throughout my life.

My father had taken me to see rugby internationals at Twickenham and to see Oxford University play on the Oxford University Ground on the Iffley road, so I was delighted to have the chance to play rugby at my new school. I was fast for my age, so I was selected to play in the school team in the first term, to play Magdalen College School at Brackley. They tried me first of all in the centre, but I was only about five stone in weight and I was no match for the big hefty fellows at Magdalen College, many of them big strong farmers' sons who were in the fifth or sixth forms. I got quite a battering in that first game, but it only made me determined to train harder. The following year I got into the first team, where I was able to stand up for myself and play a reasonable part in the game.

My last year at school was one of my most satisfying, as in the summer term I was elected cricket captain. We got together the best cricket team that the school had seen since it opened in 1924, and won matches against Banbury and Chipping Norton, although they were bigger schools. In each match we made well over 200 runs.

At the end of the school year we sat our school certificate. I was pleased to receive a note from the headmaster at the end of the school holidays saying I was one of those who had attained ten credits or more in the old Oxford local examination. That meant I was exempt from the London Matriculation Examination for admission to the London University colleges, which was very good news. I hadn't been able to apply for this as my parents couldn't afford it.

Marjorie had attended Mrs Hickman's school, a private school in

Bicester, from the age of about 11. Mrs Hickman was a well-to-do farmer's daughter who had a house in the Causeway, next to the blacksmith. My sister went there to learn music, elocution and dancing.

I remember a boy called Clifton who became a wonderful artist in oils. He painted the banner under which Bicester school paraded into Chelsea football ground before the Duke of York. He also became a master craftsman and a cabinetmaker, and I can remember him making a box camera during a woodwork class. Yet he was never entered for the scholarship.

When after the war I was giving a lecture on aircraft accident prevention, I noticed sitting in the front row a lad called Perrin who had left my school at 15. I remember the French master called him Percy Perrin, after the captain of Surrey Cricket Club. He had been awarded a scholarship, but it was the luck of the draw.

It was very competitive at the grammar school. Every Monday the headmaster read our names from the top of the form to the bottom, so we all knew how well we were doing.

I had three farmers in my class, including Ken Harrison from Luggershall, who used to hunt, and Doug Clark from Weston-on-the-Green, whose sister was the mother of Derek Hedges. He wasn't the brightest boy, but he stayed on until the year before school certificate and his brain gradually started to work better. I think he would have scraped through with about four or five subjects in the old school certificate.

Woodeaton Manor, mentioned above, was a delightful country house belonging to a Captain Wayland, who had served in a cavalry regiment. We understood that he had lost most of his fortune through horse racing, either as an unsuccessful owner or, more likely, in betting on the horses. He was forced to sell the Manor and buy a semi-detached house in Priory Road, Bicester, where he ended his days with his spinster sister, looked after by Mr Redfern, who was his valet, and Mrs Wise, a relative of the Wises in Islip, who was Captain Wayland's cook at their Bicester house. It meant that the Waylands were living in much reduced circumstances compared to their life at Woodeaton Manor.

While at Islip I also made friends with the Charlotte brothers, Richard and Herbert. When Herbert passed the exam for the county school, his father, although he was only a farm worker, was happy to provide what little money he had to enable his son to travel on the train to Bicester to attend the school.

In fact it was Richard who was the cleverer of the two brothers. Realising this, his father somehow paid for a place for him too. To save the train fare he bought him a Raleigh three-speed bicycle, which Richard rode the eight miles to school and back every day for the five years he was there. Both boys were able to repay their father's generosity later, thanks to their salaries as senior local government officers.

Islip was connected to the railway system in the 1830s, when the railway line was driven from Bletchley to Oxford via all the villages en route. There were two or three trains a day into Oxford and the same back, with the last one at nine o'clock in the evening, so they no longer had to rely on the carrier's cart which visited Oxford on Wednesdays and Saturdays.

The railway station at Islip had a large coalyard which served the coal merchants who were delivering to the Otmoor towns. It also took hay from Otmoor for the City of London stables which provided the horses for the London buses and trams. The hayricks were cut into small bundles called bales or trusses, which were compressed in a hay press. Itinerant hay tyers used to travel round the farms, where they would be paid to cut the hayricks into small rectangular packets with a big hay knife, which had a blade two feet long and nine inches wide and had to be kept very sharp.

The tyer would cut layers three feet by eighteen inches wide and six inches thick. Each layer in turn would be put into the base of the compression chamber of the hay press, and the tyer would add more layers until the truss, or bale, weighed about 56 lbs. Once he had screwed the top of the press down on to the bale, he tied the strings and removed the bale from the press. The bales were then loaded on to farm wagons and taken to Islip for transport to London.

Michael Henchard, the leading character in Thomas Hardy's The Mayor of Casterbridge, was a famous hay tyer; he sold his wife to a soldier.

Robert Graves, the writer and Oxford University professor, had bought a small house in Islip, across the river on the road towards Noke. His best-selling 1929 autobiography, Goodbye to All That, shows that he had little regard for many of the farmers in Islip, but he was full of praise for William Beckley, always known as 'Fisher' Beckley, because his forebears had assisted Cromwell during the Civil War and as a result the Beckley family had been given special fishing rights in the River Cherwell.

I knew Fisher Beckley's son Will very well. He had won a scholarship from the Islip school and was a useful member of the school rugby team.

Then there was Frank Steele from Islip, a cousin of my mother's, who became an aircraftsman in the RAF. At RAF Henlow he became the RAF heavyweight boxing champion. He once fought for the Combined Services boxing team against Oxford University and my father, and I think the foreman of Sir Lindsay Parkinson, the builders, arranged for a lorry to take some of the men into Oxford Town Hall for the match. I was able to go in on the lorry with the men and sit in the front row.

Through the late 1920s and 1930s the agricultural depression continued to deepen. The tenants of the neighbouring farm, Hawkwell Farm, where I now live, left in 1930 because it was no longer viable. The land was a thin, stony soil, known locally as "hungry land". It was Oxford stone brash, very similar to the Cotswolds. Later on in the 1950s and 60s, when we were able to de-stone it, we would collect 15 or 20 tons of stone per acre with the stone picker. When you started cultivating it you wondered where the stone was all coming from, because it still looked as bad as ever.

Hawkwell Farm had been farmed by a man called Thomas Finch for many years until it was let in 1918 at £1 per acre to a Mr W A Cattell. Mr Cattell appears to have handed it over to his son Thomas when Thomas came out of the Army at the end of the First World War. Tom Cattell was an intelligent farmer and he managed to keep it going until the depression of 1930/31. He asked the landlord for a reduction in rent of 25%, as he had kept meticulous accounts which showed that he could have scratched a living and kept the farm viable at 15 shillings an acre. But the landlord wouldn't agree to this, so Mr Cattell left.

He moved to Barndon Farm, Oddington, where the clay soil helped him to be more successful.

At Barndon, Tom Cattell started milking, which proved profitable. He went on to buy Hare Leys Farm at Launton. When Tom finally retired, Bert Evans, the son of Alf Evans, the drapers in Sheep Street, Bicester, took over the farm, and I believe Bert's son still farms there today.

Fortunately, after my paternal grandmother died in 1931, things became a little easier for my father. She left him an annual income of about £700, a third of the income from her estate. Even so, we still led quite a frugal existence.

Hawkwell Farm stayed empty until March 1931, when a Mr Richard Collett came from one of the Otmoor farms to take it on. His main reason was that it was near the County School, where he hoped to send his children. Mr Collett offered ten shillings an acre, which was accepted by the same landlord who six months earlier had refused to accept 15 shillings. This was typical of what was happening all over England, particularly with arable farms.

I always got on well with Mr Collett. He had served in the Queen's Own Oxfordshire Hussars, my father's old regiment. He had gone to France with the regiment at the outbreak of war; they were probably the first yeomanry regiment to arrive there in 1914. I enjoyed listening to his stories of his exploits.

Chapter 3

He was also a good judge of horses. In 1932 he went to Cheltenham Races with a friend of his, Roland Hawes, and was fortunate enough to back the winners of the two races which formed the Tote Double for the day. He came home with £480 in cash – enough to pay his rent at Hawkwell Farm for four years.

In about 1934 one of our neighbours was offered 40 acres of Gowell Farm rent-free for two years on condition that he ploughed it to grow wheat. But when the land had been steam-ploughed in about 1925, the huge furrow slices had been left standing. You could have broken your ankle if you'd tried to run over them. He told me he would have needed another pair of horses to undertake the work, either that or use a contractor, and he couldn't afford either. The weeds had grown up between the furrows and that's how it had stayed until 1932, when a new tenant, Mr Marlow, moved in. He was able to do it only because he had horses and a hard-working son to help him cultivate the land. That was just one example of the parlous state to which agriculture had been reduced since the First World War.

Towards the end of the 1920s we saw the first aircraft arrive at the rebuilt RAF station at Bicester. They were Hawker Horsleys, a light day bomber with a Napier Lion engine - not very fast, but a very safe aeroplane to fly, I was told. I spent many hours on my bicycle sitting by the side of the road watching them take off and land in fascination. I never dreamed, however, that one day I might fly myself.

Unfortunately the Air Ministry now needed our land at Copthall Farm for the construction of the new airfield, so we had to give up the tenancy there.

Some of the airmen and junior officers from the RAF station at Bicester joined the cricket or football clubs at Bicester, and through the cricket club I got to know one or two of the young officers. In particular I remember Flying Officer Edwards, who was later awarded the Victoria Cross for leading a daylight raid on Bremen. I also remember Flight Lieutenant

George Beamish, who, with his brother, played rugger for Ireland.

While living in Islip with me and my grandmother, my eldest sister Marjorie had met Stuart Logsdail, the son of a well-known Victorian artist who lived at The Manor, Noke. In June 1932 they got married. It was a bright sunny day with a little cloud and it wasn't as hot as we would have liked, but the ceremony was delightful and the bride and her four bridesmaids looked lovely. The reception went off very well and the bride and groom left for a holiday in Cornwall, which became their favourite holiday place. A couple of years later I joined them on holiday there.

Stuart and Marjorie went to live in the Manor Cottage, in the garden of the Manor at Noke, to which Stuart's parents had moved from Kensington some years before. I would often meet old Mr Logsdail in the lovely rose garden there. He was always ready to talk to me, even though I was still just a schoolboy. He would chat about his early days as a student painter and how he had worked at it in Antwerp, Venice and finally Taormina in Sicily. He said that although it was hard work, he had loved it.

He had once painted the monastery in Taormina - I think his grandson still has the painting - but when I went to see him in August 1943 he told me it had been bombed by the Americans because it had been the headquarters of one of the German Armies in Sicily. He said that if I could find out who the leader of the American bomber group had been, he would be only too pleased to present him with the painting. I thought it was a tall order to try and identify the man, and I also thought it was a shame to let the painting leave the country, so I didn't try very hard to find him.

That summer of 1932 I spent a lot of time with Stuart and Marjorie, who would come over to Lords Farm to play tennis. I often went fishing with Stuart. He was a good shot as well as a keen fisherman, and he would accompany me round the fields to have a crack at the rabbits.

When I left school in 1933 I had hoped to start as an articled clerk with a firm of accountants in Oxford which my headmaster had contacted.

However, this meant a down payment of 200 guineas, no salary at all for the first two years and then just £1 a week for the last three years until I got my articles. I couldn't possibly afford that, so I carried on working on the farm, even though there was very little opportunity to earn any real money, either then or in the future. Britain had three and a quarter million unemployed, and farming was still at a very low level. Even good agricultural land was only fetching about £10 an acre.

I continued to help with the milking twice a day as I had done when I was at school. It was no hardship in the morning for me to get up and milk a couple of cows before going off to school. In fact, it was delightful on a cold frosty winter's morning to pull up a stool, put a bucket under the cow and lean my head into her warm flank to start milking. It took about ten minutes to milk the two cows.

I would always get the quiet cows that didn't kick and were easy to milk. There's a great variation between cows and how quickly you can milk them. Some had large teat channels through which the milk flowed easily, while others had narrower ones which required a lot more pressure. We carried on milking by hand like this until 1945, when we installed a milking machine.

After a year or so Stuart became concerned that I wasn't getting anywhere by staying at home and relying on my farm work for spending money. He managed a garage in Merton Street for Morris Garages, so he suggested I should write to Morris Motors and ask if they had any openings for a lad like me with a good School Certificate and a decent head for maths.

I did as he suggested. I wrote and told them I didn't mind what work I did, I just wanted the chance to prove myself. I also followed his advice not to ask for a salary. The letter had the right effect, because a few days later I was called for an interview in the accounts department.

The interview went well and I was offered a job in the department, which was next to Lord Nuffield's private office. It was a very junior job of course, but to me it was a lifeline. My first wage packet was 25 shillings a week, which was only three shillings less than an agricultural worker's weekly wage. A year later it was increased to 35 shillings and after another year it went all the way up to 45 shillings, because they said I had worked well and deserved it.

Cowley is now the home of Oxford Science Park. It has certainly changed. Before the First World War Lord Nuffield was building his cars in wooden huts there.

My headmaster, John Howson, had started an Old Scholars' Loan Fund with funds raised by the staff and through the school play. The only person I knew who took advantage of it was Doris Miles, who was five years older than me. Her father was a monumental mason and a very religious man. He had a 100-gallon horse-drawn tank for paraffin and he used to bring it round to the back door and fill up my mother's lamps and stove from it. She was the first girl from the school to go to university and I believe she became quite a successful head teacher at a girls' school.

None of the boys in my year at the grammar school went to university. The first man who did go went up to Reading, to read Agriculture with Zoology. I think he might have even got a PhD. He was researching the spread of the muntjac deer which had been introduced by the Duke of Bedford at Woburn. To get to Reading in those days you had to have Latin, which wasn't on our curriculum. One boy, Joe Pickvance, stayed on a year to get his Latin higher school certificate. I remember him as a bit of a bully in the rugger team, though I could run faster than him.

On leaving school I had joined the Oxford Nomads Rugby Club, the premier rugger club in Oxford, which had been started by Ronnie Pulton-Palmer, an England international player and an Oxford graduate before the First World War. Ronnie was killed in the war, but the club flourished and I found that the members were congenial fellows, most of them from minor public schools, and I got on reasonably well with them.

By 1938 I had been playing for the county for two years and had obtained good write-ups in the national press for some of the matches. I played on the wing, and at Iffley Road I scored from opportunities created by Emrys Watkins, a brilliant fly-half, or one of the inside centres, such as Avery Rogers or W G Moseby, both of whom played in the centre for the RAF.

In 1937 I had also won the 100 yard and 200 yard sprints in the Morris Motors Sports, and had been presented with a camera and a box of fish knives and forks by Lady Nuffield. But by 1938 many of my friends in the rugger club were joining the Territorial Army, or volunteering for the Royal Air Force or the Naval Reserve. Increasingly, the talk was of war with Germany.

A farm boy goes to war
1938-39

By 1936 I had become a shipping clerk with Morris Industries Exports, who were exporting their motor cars mainly to the dominions, such as South Africa, Australia and New Zealand - they didn't want them sold on the continent or in America. One day the chief accountant at Morris Motors handed me an application form for the supplementary reserve officers for the Oxford and Bucks light infantry - he thought I might be Army officer material.

I knew that many of my friends were joining the Territorial Army, but I wasn't sure about this idea. I was now playing rugby with many members of the Royal Air Force team, including A V Rogers and Bill Moseby, who were stationed at Abingdon, and D S Kemp, stationed at Bicester. When we'd played at Abingdon, Upper Heyford or RAF Bicester, we had had a glimpse of what it was like to be in the Air Force. I thought it seemed a pretty good life.

One of the easiest ways to get into the services at the time was to take a short-service commission, which lasted four years. You could come out with £300-£400 and on top of that you'd be qualified for a job in the aviation industry, which was then starting to expand.

However, they were inundated with applicants. It was not until the following year, 1937, that I was finally given a date to appear before a selection board at Adastral House in Kingsway, London – it must have been late November. As it happens, the previous day I had been playing rugger for Oxfordshire against Berkshire and on the morning of the interview I had a glowing write-up in the national papers, thanks to a late try I had scored which had saved us from defeat. I'd been playing in the three-quarter line with H D Freakes, the South African fullback, and Richard E Luyt, another South African at Oxford. Claude Davey, who was then the Welsh captain, was on the Berkshire team, and I realised I had got the legs of Davey when he went by me in the first half, because when I turned round I found I could catch him quite easily.

When I arrived at the selection board it was all done very decently. They did everything to put the candidates at their ease - they didn't want people browbeaten or frightened. Before the interview an officer went through my history - birth, schooling, further education and jobs. He was more interested in my rugger than anything else, as he had seen the headlines about the previous day's match.

The interview was very short. One of the panel did ask me about the function of the differential on a motor car, and of course after two or three years at Morris Motors I knew something of how a car worked. But most of the time was taken up talking about my sports - football, hockey, cricket, tennis, shooting, and fishing.

If they sent you for a medical, you knew you'd been selected. They gave me a ticket for one, and that same afternoon I went off in high spirits on the Tube to Warren Street. Unfortunately, I had a sore throat, because we'd done so much singing the night before at the rugger match – and they turned me down. They told me I had passed everything else, but I would have to come back in a few weeks when the throat was better.

It didn't work out quite like that. The following Boxing Day I was asked to play rugby down at Lydney on the River Severn. Graham Parker, the English fullback, tackled me and I injured my right knee. That was the end of my match, and my season. When I finally went for a second medical, I had to cover up a bad limp. I got away with it and passed, but that knee has bothered me ever since.

My decision to join the Royal Air Force did not go down well with my parents. My father, who had seen so many aircraft shot down over the

Somme in 1916-18, was well aware of the high casualties among flying personnel in those old planes. My brother-in-law Stuart had lost his brother through a flying accident at RAF Kenley in 1926. My father worried my mother by suggesting that I would not last long in the RAF, particularly now that war was on the horizon.

By this time there was a young lady in my life. Daphne Dickins was the daughter of the farmer at Bignell Park Farm. We had met in 1936, playing tennis in Bicester (there were eight of us, four girls and four young men). Her father would come past on his bike and say, "Daphne, it's time you came home". The following year I was brave enough to invite them to come and play on our tennis court at Lords Farm. I didn't realise the girls had romantic designs on us boys. I was very innocent – I invited only male friends to my 21st birthday party!

On Saturdays, which were half days, I would wait in Catte Street, near the Radcliffe Camera in Oxford, to pick Daphne up from Barclays Bank and drive her home in my MG. We used to go and watch the night flying at Upper Heyford, which was really just an opportunity for a squeeze. I always had to get her home in good time. In November 1937 I took her to the Farmers' Ball. So when it was time for me to leave to join the RAF in April 1938, it was Daphne who helped me to pack my trunk.

I began my basic training at the De Havilland School of Flying in Hatfield on Monday April 4th 1938, but I hadn't finished on the farm just yet. I remember that the day before I was due to report to Hatfield, I had some chain harrowing to finish. When we got down to the bottom of Lords Lane the horses stopped at the hedge and looked over, because they had seen someone on a horse. It turned out to be Cecil Bonner, exercising a steeplechaser. He stopped and told me that Mr Nicholson from Bucknell had won the foxhunters' steeplechase at Liverpool, so that's another date which connects with my memory of joining the RAF.

In the evening I went into Hatfield with Albert Buckle and his mate (they were the first and second whips with the Bicester Hounds) and bought them a steak and chips apiece at the Peahen Hotel in St Albans. It would have been about three shillings at that time for a steak and chips. Then they dropped me off in Hatfield.

Our mess for our two-month training period was a big house on the edge of the De Havilland airfield. After I had signed on, I was told to go over to the pub across the road, the Comet, where I would find some chaps who had already checked in. I went over there and introduced myself.

The men were all New Zealanders. When I said I came from Oxfordshire, one of the men asked if I knew the Bagnells who farmed near Burford, because they were his ancestors; his name was Doug Bagnell. I told them I did know the family and that they now farmed next to my sister at Noke, near Islip.

Doug Bagnell went on to become a successful bomber pilot and won the DFC, American DFC and DSO. He didn't get beyond Wing Commander, though. He was intelligent, but he was also very arrogant and he would never listen to anybody else, even his senior officer. You don't get promoted if you keep telling your CO he doesn't know what he's talking about.

They posted Doug to an American jet squadron as a liaison officer, and he spent the rest of his career flying jets. They seemed to spend most of their time flying to Italy or Algiers to pick up booze and duty-free gifts from their 'PX'. When he retired he bought a yacht and chartered it in the Caribbean, but it lost a lot of money.

We were divided into two squads of 28-30 men. One squad would fly in the morning and the other in the afternoon. The one that wasn't flying would be undertaking ground school: navigation, engineering, airmanship, aeronautics, ballistics, gunnery. I think all the New Zealanders had flown, or had had some instruction. They had already had their medicals in New Zealand, so they knew they weren't going to be failed on that when they got to England, but I think they had to pay for their passage. I remember these boys had come on a cargo ship through the Panama Canal.

Some of the group were boys straight from school, and there was an ex-police cadet and a couple of men who had been in the Army and decided to transfer. At that time anyone could transfer from one of the armed forces to flying training in the RAF, because it was so important to get pilots under training to meet the threat of war.

We learned about airmanship, the theory of flight, meteorology, aircraft engines, armaments and navigation. The young school-leavers had a slight advantage over us older men and seemed to cope easily with the mathematics required for navigation, aircraft engines and armaments. However, I managed to pass out in the top third of the course.

There were three members of our group that failed to make the grade. They had set their hearts on flying, but they all had to return to civilian life.

It was a very well-run flying school, with good discipline. We were flying the de Havilland Tiger Moth, a delicate little aircraft which was very easy to fly but it showed up all your faults, so it was a good trainer. Once you could land a Tiger Moth neatly you could manage the other aircraft that you'd have to deal with later. I found that flying straight and level is a piece of cake – it's the landing that's the difficult part.

My daughter Marijoy found flying easy, I think. In 1968, while living in Harborne, Birmingham, she won a flying lesson in a 'Train With Wills' competition organised by W D & H O Wills, the tobacco company. She learned to fly before she passed her driving test.

I had been driving a little MG – it was cheaper for travelling than the train – but when I started at Hatfield I was advised not to bring it with me. I soon found out why. One night I left it in the car park of the Comet. As we were leaving one chap offered to take it back. He and another fellow got in and drove off, and they hadn't gone 200 yards when they hit the kerb and buckled the inside wheel. They were right, you couldn't trust any of these RAF officers. I was able to drive it back, but the axle was badly damaged.

Chapter 4

The next stage was a fortnight's disciplinary training at Uxbridge, where we did foot drills and rifle drill on the parade ground. There was a lot of early-morning physical training, and our hair had to be trimmed short. We paraded in sports jackets, flannel trousers and black shoes, which had to be highly polished. We had to attend the colour-hoisting parade at 8 o'clock and afterwards continued with foot drill until midday, when we were allowed to have lunch.

I found the foot drill and rifle drill no hardship. In fact I thoroughly enjoyed it. It was like being part of a rugger team - you did exactly what you were told. Many of my colleagues could not see the point, but I enjoyed it all.

Finally the time came for us to be fitted out with our new uniforms. We were given a list of tailors in the West End who could make decent RAF uniforms, and invited to choose from the list. Gieves was far and away the most popular, but they soon became oversubscribed, so many of us turned to other tailors, who proved to be equally good.

On completion of the two weeks of training we were commissioned – it would have been about June 4. We were then told to go by train to RAF Sealand near Chester, where we would start training on service-type aircraft. Sealand was the home of the No. 5 Service Flying Training School. Here we were joined forces with pupils from two other elementary flying schools, so there were now 60 or 70 of us.

We flew the Hawker Audax, which was a two-seater light bomber with a 600 horsepower Rolls-Royce Kestrel engine and an air-gunner in the back. Most of us also trained on the Hawker Hart, which was used for dual instruction. None of us found much difficulty in converting from the little Tiger Moth to the very much larger and much more powerful Hart, which had been introduced into the service in 1930 and was still being used in Egypt and India for operational duties.

In the senior term some of those who had trained on the Hart were transferred to the Hawker Fury, which entered service in 1931. This was a single-engined biplane, though still a very popular aircraft. It was a good trainer for pilots who were destined for fighter squadrons, which were now re-equipping with Hawker Hurricanes and Supermarine Spitfires. Some of the older trainees were selected to train on the new twin-engined Airspeed Oxford, to prepare them for Bomber Command.

At first when we went to Sealand we weren't allowed cars, so I sold my little MG. Eventually I used the money to buy a Morris Eight.

It was a tradition at Sealand that soon after arriving, the junior team would hold a boxing match. The NCO PT instructors paired us up by size and weight, and into the ring we went. All the officers were there with their wives. It was like a gladiatorial contest - three two-minute rounds I think. After the third bout, two of the chaps got together and agreed not to hit each other too hard when they got into the ring, but the Group Captain soon stopped that and made them fight properly. I suppose they wanted to see the fighting spirit.

When it was my turn I had to take on a very fit-looking New Zealander. I thought I would take a beating, but I found I could hit him a lot quicker than he could hit me, and they stopped the fight in the second round. I was awarded a propelling pencil. That evening two young boxers suffered slight concussion, so a higher authority decided that there should be no more boxing for trainee pilots.

I was at Sealand for six months, and it was a very comfortable existence. We started off at half past seven, straight after breakfast, by marching about a quarter of a mile to the armoury, where we drew rifles. Then we had about 20 minutes' rifle drill before going on colour-hoisting parade at eight o' clock with the whole of the station personnel.

For our armament training at the end of our course we had to move to RAF Penrhos, near Pwllheli in North Wales, to practise bombing targets in the sea and front-gun attacks on ground targets. We flew in pairs, taking turns as pilot and bomb-aimer. I was using my propelling pencil to make notes on a mission one day when I dropped it out of the aircraft, right over the middle of Liverpool. I was afraid it would hit somebody on the head and go straight through them, but I think I got away with it.

Three chaps on our course didn't make the grade and were rusticated. One chap I felt dreadfully sorry for, because he seemed to be making good progress. But he had great difficulty making a neat landing, so he was chucked out.

About once every three weeks we were detailed to undertake the post of duty pilot. That meant sitting in the watch office or flying control tower with the duty pilot, who was there to record all the arrivals and departures and make sure that flying procedures and discipline on the ground were followed correctly, because of the large numbers of aircraft that would be operating at any one time.

After three months we had completed the first part of our course and had to sit written examinations. They were not too difficult and I passed out, I'm glad to say, in the top half of the course. Again it was the younger members who had been at school more recently who seemed to cope better with the written examinations, and some of the very young ones proved to be quick to become effective pilots.

Two of our pilots had not done sufficiently well to qualify for the flying badge. They were told that they couldn't go on leave yet – they would have to retake their exams before they could get their badges.

In September 1938, halfway through our course, we were given a week's leave. Doug Bagnell came with me. I took him to meet his long-lost relations at Noke, and we went to Blenheim Palace. But the visit was cut short when a policeman arrived at Lords Farm with a note telling us to report back to Sealand immediately.

When we arrived there the padre told us that we had to start the next stage of our training without delay, because we would shortly be posted to a squadron. It looked as if war was imminent. The next morning we were told that the rest of our training would probably be condensed to a month, as we were urgently required in frontline squadrons.

I remember how horrified the senior officers on the station were that Czechoslovakia was going to be sacrificed to settle the Munich Crisis, as it came to be known. They felt that abandoning Czechoslovakia would not stop Hitler, and of course they were right. Hitler had said it was his last claim in Europe, but we had not yet realised what a master of deceit he was. I felt so strongly about the sacrifice of Czechoslovakia that when my son John went on a rugby tour to the Czech Republic in 1997, I wrote a speech of apology for him to deliver at his post-match dinners.

In the event the crisis was settled (not very satisfactorily) by the Prime Minister, Neville Chamberlain, which at least allowed us to continue our flying training with a little less pressure.

Towards the end of the course we were asked to choose which branch of the RAF we would like to enter - Bombing, Fighter, Coastal Command or Army Co-operation Command. I found it difficult to choose between Fighter Command and Army Co-operation Command, but my instructor pointed out to me that Fighter Command would keep me on a fighter station somewhere in the south east, whereas Army Co-operation Command offered the chance to operate overseas, in the Middle East or on the north-west frontier in India. This sounded attractive to me. He also told me that if you applied for Fighter Command and didn't get it, you might be posted to other duties that you wouldn't necessarily like, but if you applied for Army Co-operation Command it was likely you'd get in as they were still looking for pilots to man the squadrons that would go overseas with the Army if war broke out as we all expected.

Army Co-operation Squadrons in those days were manned by a mixture of Army officers who had been trained to fly by the RAF and were to serve four years with the RAF and stay with them in the event of war.

By Christmas we had completed most of our training, but we did have to return after the holiday for the final few days. We had a passing-out parade before being told where we would be posted. I and about half a dozen others were told we were going to the Army Co-operation School (ACS) at Old Sarum near Salisbury, as we were destined to go to Army Co-operation Squadrons. I had looked forward to this as I had hoped I might end up in India, in the NW frontier somewhere near Peshawar, or it might have been Iraq or even Egypt.

The day we passed out, a dinner was held for us. It was rather like a service dinner, as an introduction to what it would be like dining-in in a regular RAF mess.

My application to be trained as an Army co-operation pilot was confirmed and, in January 1939, I was posted to the School of Army Co-operation. I reported with about eight of my fellow trainee officers to their headquarters at RAF Old Sarum, near Salisbury. Here we were expected to transmit all our messages from the air by W/T (wireless telegraphy) in morse code. Fortunately, this was something which I had practised very hard at in my early days at senior flying training school, when Bagnell and I would transmit messages by Morse code to test each other.

We were expected to learn to transmit at 40 words a minute and receive and write down messages at 20 wpm, which we found easy. I had to learn to transmit with my right hand, because the key in the aircraft was on the right and I would be flying with my left hand on the control panel. This was no problem for me, as I'm left-handed.

We were trained in various forms of aerial photography - low-level, eye-level and oblique. With oblique photography we might be taking images anywhere from 50 feet above the ground up to 4000 feet, which would give you a better view, for example, of the line of a river or road. The Williamson F.24 camera we used was a very bulky piece of equipment which was controlled from the cockpit by an electrical switch which allowed us to time the exposures and the interval between them.

We were trained to be precise and accurate in reporting the positions of enemy or allied forces or any defence fortifications in our reconnaissance area. We used three-letter codes, such as INF for Infantry, HDT for Horse-Drawn Transport and AFV for Armoured Fighting Vehicles. We were taught where to look for enemy guns, which would normally be at the edges of woods or behind hills, and to give an accurate six-figure reference point so that British guns could be brought to bear on the enemy within a few seconds of our reporting their positions from the air.

We spent nearly three months at Old Sarum, and it was a delightful period in our training. It was hard to believe we were being paid sixteen shillings and sixpence a day for what we had to do. The mess at Old Sarum was the best I had experienced. Breakfast was a feast - there were always prunes or other fruit for breakfast, whitebait and kippers, sausages, eggs and bacon, kidneys, tomatoes, mushrooms and hot crusty rolls. Lunch was of the same high standard. There was always a large roast joint on a hotplate which was carved in front of you by one of the chefs.

We had a few days' leave before the end of the course, so my sister Joan and my mother drove down to Old Sarum to collect me and take me back to the farm. I was glad to see that Harry Jennings and Alf Bannister were both doing an excellent job for my father. At busy times, when Harry and Alf got behind, my father was able to enlist the help of a local agricultural contractor who had invested in an Austin tractor. He would take on any ploughing or heavy cultivating which was needed.

After the land had been ploughed it was fairly easy to break down the furrow slices with a pair of horses pulling heavy harrows. The tines in the last row, called duck's foot tines, were curved inwards at the bottom to drag any squitch (the local name for couch grass) to the top. They pulled through the stubble about five inches under the ground. At the end of the field the driver of the horses would lift the drags to let the rhizomes of the squitch fall from the tines. They would then be left in a heap at the edge of the field to be burned. A small heap of squitch would burn for a month,

making a rather pleasant smoky smell that would drift across the field on
an early autumn morning.

I've often wondered why, after the war, the term 'squitch' was allowed
to fall into disuse. The same thing applied to the yellow plant that grew
profusely on this land and was always known as cerlick. That name in the
1930s was changed to charlock. I often wondered why they couldn't hang
on to the old names.

By 1938 the Government, anxious about the state of our wheat reserves
and the possibility of the interruption of wheat supplies across the Atlantic
in the event of war, had introduced a grant of £2 an acre to plough
grassland up for wheat. This enabled some farmers to make better use of
some of their old grassland, but not everyone could afford the cost of the
ploughing.

Pulling heavy drags was a good way of breaking in a young horse to
fieldwork. When I was a child the carters would do this by harnessing the
young horse in between two older animals. All three of them would be in
trace harness, that is they would have chains from their collars which were
attached to every drag, so three swingle trees would accommodate three
horses. The young horse in the middle would adapt itself to the pace of
the two older horses on either side of it, and it could be broken in in a day.

Young horses could be a danger to themselves and to people working
with them unless they were properly and carefully broken. In the summer
of 1938 we had a serious accident in the hayfields at Lords Farm. A young
horse which my father had bought was put into a horse rake to rake the
hayfield on Hill Ground. Because it was only partially broken, Harry
Jennings was to ride the hay rake and hold the reins while Alfie Bannister
was to lead the horse until it got used to the clanking noise as the rake
lifted and the tines fell back on to the ground.

On this particular day, Alfie was detailed to lead the horse up and down
the field for half an hour or so to get it used to the work in the shafts and
the noise. But as they started off the horse was startled, perhaps by a fly

or a wasp, and it started forward very fast. Alfie, taken by surprise, fell alongside the horse. He was caught up in the tines of the horse-rake and began to be raked up with the hay. Harry leaned forward to lift up the rake and pressed with his right foot, but he too was unseated from the rather unstable seat above the horse-rake. He fell down in front of the rake, and there were now two men being raked up as the horse cantered towards the far hedge.

Fortunately the hedge was only about 60 yards away, and when the horse reached it it stopped and began to graze the fresh green grass under the hedge bottom. This allowed both Alfie and Harry to extricate themselves from the rake. Harry was unhurt, but Alfie had severe gashes on his back. Harry would often relate how, when they both pulled themselves from the horse-rake and sat by the horse's head, Alfie turned to him and said: "Give me my last fag mate, afore I die".

The gashes on Alfie's back didn't need stitching. He was taken to the doctors by my father and he was back at work the next day, but it was an indication of how careful one had to be when working with horses and of how dangerous farm work could be if care wasn't exercised at all times.

We did have a fatal accident at a farm only a mile away in Bucknell, where the tenant of Home Farm, George Eustace, had been loading hay prior to roping it for the journey to a neighbouring farm which had bought it. When George had finished on the top of the load, he grabbed a rope thrown by one of the workers and started to pull it up. For some reason the rope broke or came loose, and George pitched over backwards off the load. He landed on the back of his head and was killed. This was a tragic example of the dangers of not taking proper care on a farm.

I had always felt a little guilty at leaving the farm, so it was reassuring to find that the work was going so well and that my father had two reliable men to help him.

Not all the young men who could have joined up at the time did so. The importance of farming to the war effort was such that if you were a farmer you could be exempt from war service, and I knew of many successful farming families who chose not to send their sons to war. One local family had four sons, none of whom joined up.

Others, by contrast, couldn't wait to get into uniform. The Nicholsons at Bucknell had two sons serving with the Oxfordshire and Buckinghamshire Light Infantry while their youngest served with the RAF. The Ancils from Stud Farm at Middleton Stoney had a son in the Fleet Air Arm, and the Gosses at Stratton Audley also had a son called up. Mr Ridgeway at Bucknell had an only son who joined the Royal Navy as soon as war was declared.

I wasn't the only Malins to serve – my sister Nellie served in the WAAF (Women's Auxiliary Air Force) and was later commissioned.

One particularly sad example was a young man named Roy Berry, who became an honorary member of the officers' mess at RAF Windrush and was so enraptured with life there that he couldn't wait to leave his family farm in the care of his mother and become a bomber pilot. He was killed over Germany on his first operational flight.

The landed gentry and minor aristocracy in the Bicester area also seemed to have a strong sense of duty. Colonel Wyndham of Caversfield sent his two sons off to the war, and one was killed. He also lost three brothers in the First World War - one more and he would have inherited the peerage and become Lord Leckinfield. Sir Algernon Peyton, Baronet, also lost his son during the war, which was the end of the baronetcy.

Mr Budget, Master of the Bicester Fox Hounds, sent both his Oxford-educated sons off in the early weeks of the war. The Ruck-Keene family had four sons in the armed forces, and thee of them were killed in action. Squire Hoare from Bignell lost his only son in World War I and four grandsons (also of the Ruck-Keene family) in World War II. It was a grim tally.

It was spring 1939 when I returned to Old Sarum for the completion of my course. There was no passing-out parade, but we were given a list of our scores on the course. Once again I can only claim to have been in the top half. At the top was a youngster of about 19 called Basil Jones, who had been attending a County School in Surrey, where the curriculum had been almost exactly the same as mine at the Old Grammar School in Bicester. Basil had a good brain, was very fit and an excellent swimmer.

The chap at the bottom of the list had been granted a regular commission because he was a Cambridge graduate. This showed that there were any number of youngsters from ordinary schools who could compete on level terms with Cambridge graduates.

We now had to choose a squadron, and again I pursued my plan to try to get a posting to India, where we would be flying rather antiquated aircraft up on the north-west frontier, either from Peshawar or Risalpur, or some of the remote landing grounds in the Afghan Hills. In the event I was posted to No.4 Squadron at Odiham in Hampshire, so my hopes of seeing the world were dashed, at least for the time being.

There was plenty of excitement ahead, just the same.

Flying operations in France – the 'phoney war'
1939-1940

I arrived at RAF Odiham in a car driven by George Grant-Govern, who had been posted to No.II(AC) Squadron at Hawkinge. George had been a great friend of mine at flying training school and I had played a little golf with him. His golf was extraordinary for a youngster – in fact he was the last RAF golf champion before the outbreak of war in 1939.

His family owned a rather palatial house next to the golf course at Wimbledon, and I had stayed with him there. His father had been the chairman, I think, of Indian National Airways, which then became Tata Airways. George Grant-Govern was killed in a flying accident towards the end of the war; a very sad affair, because he was an only son and his parents doted on him.

On arrival at RAF Odiham we were shown to our rooms and a batman was assigned to look after us, one batman to two or three junior officers. We had big, comfortable rooms, each with a single bed, a washbasin and a small desk. The next day we reported to the adjutant of No.4 Squadron in the hangar, who marched the six of us off to meet the Commanding Officer, Major I. O. B. McGregor. There were two other squadrons at Odiham – No.13, equipped with Westland Lysanders, and No.59, which had long-nosed Bristol Blenheim light bombers for long-range reconnaissance.

It was just as well I had begun to lose my childhood nickname of Major by that time. It wouldn't have gone down well to be known to your mates as Major when your CO was a real major. Old McGregor must have thought he was still in the Army, because he carried on wearing khaki and seemed to prefer being known as Major, rather than Squadron Leader.

McGregor was a former inter-services boxing champion, and he was tough. He was also arrogant and conceited. On that first introduction, he simply ignored us. In fact, he carried on ignoring us. I don't think he spoke to any of us that whole summer.

He also had a much higher opinion of his own flying abilities than they deserved. That August, he lost command of the Squadron because of a serious flying accident. He demanded to be put on the night-flying programme, so at short notice the officer in charge of night flying notified his Squadron that an aircraft was to be made available for him around 9 pm. McGregor took off as night was falling, and after about half an hour in the air he returned to the airfield to make a landing. But he misjudged his final approach and hit the hedge. The impact turned the aircraft on to its back and left him upside down inside the aircraft. The engine was torn away from its mounting by the rotation of the propeller and McGregor was left sitting upside down in the cockpit with his engine a few yards away.

The injuries he received might have killed a man who was not so fit or tough, but they seemed to have little effect on McGregor. Within a few weeks he was back in the mess.

McGregor was replaced by Squadron Leader Guy Charles, from No.16 Squadron, who was a great improvement. Charles had earned the Sword of Honour at Cranwell. He was a great fellow - the sort of chap who would go up to you in the bar and offer to buy you a drink. He might say, "Have you had any?" and if you said you'd had three he'd say "Well that's enough, I'm not going to buy you another!"

Charles brought with him from No.16 Squadron Flight Lieutenant Bill Maffett, an Army officer seconded from the Duke of Wellington's Regiment, and Flying Officer Wally Barton, a Canadian. Wally Barton was an excellent pilot and a fine fellow to have in the Squadron. Bill Maffett was a keen aviator, but we never thought too highly of his ability.

He had been trained at Sandhurst and eventually joined the regiment his father had served in. I'm sorry to say that Bill, Wally and Guy would all be killed before the end of the war.

The summer of 1939 at Odiham was very pleasant. I went sailing with a friend down at Bosham, and we played cricket and tennis. Of course, it couldn't last. On Sunday September 3, a week or two before Squadron Leader Charles joined us, war was declared with Germany.

I heard the news that morning as I was passing the batmen's room and one of them invited me in to listen to his radio because the Prime Minister was about to make a speech. We heard Chamberlain's voice telling us he had warned Hitler that unless the German troops were withdrawn from Poland within 24 hours, Britain would consider itself at war with Germany. The 24 hours was now up.

"What will happen to us now, sir?" asked the batman. I told him we would be sent to an airfield somewhere in France, but I had no idea which one.

Before leaving for France I phoned home to tell them what was happening and to ask my sister Joan to collect my little Morris Eight, which I had only bought a few months earlier. When she arrived the next day to collect it, she was told that one of the officers had borrowed it. This, I'm afraid, was rather typical of the Royal Air Force. My sister had to wait a couple of hours for the fellow who had taken it to turn up before driving it back to Bicester.

We had about 80 First World War reservists at Odiham. Most of them had been working as drivers for London Transport. Many had become MT (motor transport) drivers or fitters. MT drivers would do five to seven years in the RAF, some of them ten as it would give them a little extra pay. There were also the supplementary reserves, for men who had not been in the armed forces. Being a mobile Squadron we had to be able to move quickly, so we had a large number of vehicles, old Crossleys built in the

1920s. Vehicles weren't discarded and replaced as they are today, they were just maintained and kept going indefinitely. It was remarkable how those Crossleys lasted, but they were difficult to start in cold weather.

It was a clear, sunny day when we took off for the flight across the English Channel. We were flying the new Westland Lysander, which was intended to be the new operational aircraft for Army Co-operation. The "Lizzie" had an 890 horsepower Bristol Mercury Engine, no armour plating, no self-sealing fuel tanks, and by any standard it was slow. To stay alive, we would have to see the enemy first and fly as low as possible. There were two front guns, while the air gunner in the back was armed with a Lewis gun. We were loaded up with tool boxes and other equipment, so my aircraft was slightly unstable when flying in loose formation.

As we flew out into the Channel I thought I could see the Seven Sisters, the famous white cliffs, away to the east. I had walked to the Seven Sisters with my father's cousin, Herbert McFarlane, a few years before, when I had stayed in the house they had rented for a holiday. Herbert had fought in the First World War with the Middlesex Regiment. I thought of that delightful walk and wondered if I would ever see those cliffs a third time. In the event, it would happen sooner than I expected.

We were told to fly to Le Tréport, on the Channel coast a few miles west of the Somme, and from Le Tréport inland to Amiens. We then followed a very straight road east until we ended up at a large First World War airfield near the village of Monchy-Lagache, six miles south of Péronne. It was a pleasant little village with a stream running through it. This was to be our base. We were joined there by No.13 Squadron, while No.53 Blenheim Squadron was sent to an airfield near Poix, about 40 miles away.

This was the period that came to be known as the 'phoney war'. Our squadrons were engaged in exercises with the Army which involved making strategic withdrawals of large units up to brigade or even divisional level, and advancing units to take up defensive positions ready for an attack on some particular objective. All this we found very interesting, but it did seem that our training was never going to end.

That autumn proved to be a remarkably pleasant few months, ended only by the arrival of very cold weather at the end of November. The snow and frost prevailed until Christmas Day, which was a jolly affair. In keeping with RAF tradition, the officers served Christmas dinner to the other ranks and NCOs in the Salle des Fêtes, the village hall.

The mixture of Army uniforms added a good deal of colour to our mess activities, particularly on dining-in night, when all the Army officers appeared in their regimental evening dress. Their scarlet and gold contrasted with the rather restrained blue of the RAF uniforms and made a delightful and colourful spectacle at these events.

In mid December we were told that all aircrew would be given short periods of leave of up to ten days. One evening all our names went into a hat to decide who would be going when. I was lucky enough to draw the period starting on Boxing Day. I left Monchy-Lagache at four o'clock in the afternoon, passing deep snow on both sides of the road, to catch the Boulogne train from Amiens. A ship was to take us from there to England.

When we arrived at the railway station, we were told that the train was delayed and that we would not be leaving until midnight. The waiting room had no fire, though we had greatcoats to keep us warm. There must have been about 20 of us there of all ranks. The train finally arrived at two in the morning and we got to Boulogne at about seven.

Once on board ship we found it a good deal warmer and we were able to make ourselves comfortable and get a bit of sleep before the ship sailed for Folkestone. The crossing took two or three hours. We finally arrived at Victoria Station quite early the following morning and took a train to Paddington. I was home in Bicester in time for tea.

It was just as cold in England as it had been in France. Thanks to some skates I had acquired when I'd been skating at the old Oxford ice rink with Stuart Logsdail, I was able to join the local farmers who were out skating on the lake at Kirtlington Park. The freeze continued during the whole period of my leave.

Chapter 5

On a warmer note, I was reunited with Daphne that Christmas holiday, and found that absence had indeed made the heart grow fonder. We started seeing each other more regularly, whenever I could get home on leave.

On returning to my Squadron at Monchy-Lagache, I was told to prepare to take my aircraft to Lille Ronchin airfield, our advance landing ground on the outskirts of the northern city of Lille, where aircraft would be sent if hostilities broke out. A flight from No.26 Squadron had been there since the start of the war, but now our Squadron was to take over.

Lille Ronchin was a very small airfield, surrounded to the north east by a maze of railway lines and on two other sides by factories and workers' houses. This meant that great care had to be used when flying into the airfield and taking off, so it was only suited to the more experienced pilots.

We found the airfield covered with a thin dusting of snow, and it was freezing hard. The B Flight mess was at flat no. 133 Rue de Douai, about 300 yards from the airfield, an easy walk in the morning along a busy street and then across a grass paddock to the hangar and offices of the old Lille Aeroclub.

Soon after arriving at Lille Ronchin we had a further heavy fall of snow, so we did little flying for the next few days. When we finally got airborne we began our work of taking photographs of the frontier between France and Belgium, and in particular the defences which were being built by the British Army on the French side.

It was a very pleasant existence, with just enough flying to keep us interested. And of course the fleshpots of Lille were only a short taxi ride away. The nightlife was not very expensive because the rate of exchange was very much in our favour - 176 francs to the pound, as I recall.

We were soon joined by two new pilots, Pilot Officer Scott and Pilot Officer Peter Peace. They had both been trained originally as fighter pilots, but had been transferred against their will to Army co-operation work. They proved to be excellent pilots. Peter Peace celebrated his 21st birthday while we were there and he organised an excellent party for the occasion, ensuring that plenty of drink was brought up and arranging with our two cooks for a sumptuous meal to be prepared.

We were also joined at about this time by Major Packe, who was originally commissioned in the Oxfordshire and Bucks Light Infantry and had transferred to the Royal Flying Corps in the First World War. After being awarded a DFC and an MBE, he returned to regimental duties. He was compulsorily retired in 1926 as a result of the Geddes Act, which led to scores of Army officers being placed on the retired list.

Packe was our guest of honour at the birthday party, along with three young French ladies who had been friends of the Squadron for the previous three or four months. They participated enthusiastically in our games of strip poker and didn't mind a bit if they lost. Those girls clearly believed in the saying "if you've got them, flaunt them"!

It was a hilarious party and Major Packe said that we had gone much further than anything he had seen in the First World War. Fortunately he said he would not report the celebration to our CO in case it led to some of us getting into trouble.

B Flight remained at Lille Ronchin until early May 1940, when we were ordered to return to Monchy-Lagache. We were to be replaced by A Flight. When we arrived at Monchy-Lagache we flew in tight formation over the village to announce to our friends there that No.4 Squadron had returned. We then embarked on more training, including night flying, which we had been unable to do from the little airfield at Lille Ronchin. We also practised dive-bombing and low-level bombing on the range at Croix-Moligneaux, a satellite airfield about five miles from Monchy.

On the morning of May 10, as I was walking from my billet on the edge of the village to the officers' mess for breakfast, I was picked up by the adjutant in his little French van. He had just heard that the Germans had started an attack across the Belgian frontier, and thought we should be in action later that day, so there was no time to lose. We flew our aircraft to Croix-Moligneaux, because we expected to be bombed at any time and we didn't want to have all the planes sitting in one field. I was detailed by the CO to ensure there would be fuel and ammunition available there for the aircraft if it was needed.

The next morning I was awakened very early by the guard. I went outside the hut in time to see a German twin-engine reconnaissance plane flying very low along the river Somme, about a mile away. It was obviously reconnoitring, perhaps to check on bridges and possible crossing places for the German troops now advancing into France.

On May 11 the CO ordered me to fly back to Lille Ronchin to join half the Squadron at the advance landing ground. He said he would be moving into Belgium to try to find a field nearer Brussels so that we could give closer support to the British forces which, he told me, would be moving up to the River Dyle, considered a formidable tank obstacle, under Plan D. So secret was the planning in the few months before the German invasion of France that none of us junior officers had even heard of Plan D.

On May 12 I carried out two reconnaissances to check how far the British forces had reached in their advance towards the river Dyle. Some had already got there, and I could see some activity along the west bank. That night the Army Intelligence Officer and the Squadron's second-in-command, Bill Maffett, warned me that I would have to undertake a sortie at first light. In the morning the intelligence officer told me that the German vanguard on the British front had still not been located, so it was up to me to try to find them.

I was briefed to fly via Brussels to Louvain and follow the main road from Louvain to Tirlemont. If I still had enough fuel, I should continue as far east as possible in the hope of locating the advancing Germans.

As I approached an area where I thought Germans might be moving,

Chapter 5

I decided to increase my speed. I climbed to 3000 feet before putting the nose down and going into a shallow dive round the south of Tirlemont to follow the road to St Trond. I then changed course to follow the road and railway line which led to St Trond. I was now flying low at my maximum speed of about 240 miles an hour.

After a few miles, I ran into what was obviously the reconnaissance unit of the German vanguard. It consisted of motorcycles and side-cars, each side-car carrying a soldier with a machine-gun. We rounded into the rising sun, which was blinding their gunners and made our attack. My air gunner, L A C Drewitt, let fly with his .303 machine-gun.

The Germans were astonished to see an aircraft flying so low and so fast – they had obviously not heard my engine, possibly because there was a slight east wind to carry the sound away. Many of them leapt out of their vehicles into the ditches.

The motorcyclists appeared to be accompanying an armoured personnel carrier of some sort, carrying German troops. I zoomed along the column, flying at times below tree level, for about four miles before turning away to port and regaining height, then set off for Army headquarters at Sottegen. Here I dropped a message in a coloured message pad and saw it picked up by a boy scout, who took it into what I presumed was an advanced headquarters tent. I then increased speed to the maximum because I thought it was important to get the news back to the Squadron as soon as possible.

When I got back, the Army intelligence officers would not believe that I had seen Germans. They suggested that the troops I saw had been retreating Belgian soldiers. I replied that if they were Belgian soldiers, they were wearing German helmets. Drewitt was an intelligent man, and he confirmed that, as he put it, he could almost have reached out and touched the heads of the Germans as I flew across the column.

The intelligence men were still reluctant to believe my story. They did not see how the Germans could have reached that position so early in the morning.

They decided to send out another aircraft to check. Pilot Officer Peter Vaughan, who had joined the Squadron only a few weeks before, was detailed to fly to the spot where I had seen the convoy. Of course, he had to allow for the fact that by the time he got there they would be 20 miles away.

Peter Vaughan and his air gunner did not return. They were shot down, either by ground fire or enemy aircraft, very close to the position where I had seen the Germans; they lie buried in a village churchyard about four miles away.

My own aircraft had been hit too. I had no idea until the fitter showed me two bullets embedded in the engine. Drewitt found another, in his parachute pack. We had had a narrow escape. On top of that our petrol tank was not equipped with the thick coverings introduced later, which would have prevented leakage in the event of a bullet piercing the petrol tank. Neither did we have the armour plate which was fitted to replacement aircraft.

We had no R/T (radio telephone) communication between pilot and air gunner. All we had was two pieces of rope attached to the top of the pilot's harness at his shoulder; the air gunner would pull one if we were attacked. If the aircraft was coming from the port quarter, he would tug on the left-hand rope, if from the starboard quarter he would pull the right. The pilot could then take immediate evasive action by going into a steep turning dive all the way to treetop height before pulling out at the last second. A German fighter, because of its cleaner silhouette, would be unable to pull out as quickly as the Lysander and would be in danger of crashing into the ground or into the tree-tops.

In the ensuing battle as the British Expeditionary Force withdrew to Dunkirk over the next few days, the Squadron flew almost non-stop. We accumulated 104 dangerous reconnaissance and dive-bombing sorties over . enemy-held positions, losing both aircraft and crews.

The next morning, May 14, I was once again detailed to undertake a dawn sortie. The intelligence officers had realised that the Germans I had seen must be closing in on the river Dyle.

As I approached the river I could see in the distance a line of German soldiers scurrying like ants along the edge of a wood, obviously hoping to lessen the chances of being observed. Again I started to lose height, but as I crossed the river immediately south of the town of Louvain I felt a vibration on the control column and realised that a bullet had hit my aileron. This was making the aircraft fly with its port wing low. I could still maintain control of the aircraft by keeping the control column far over to the right, so I decided to return home rather than risk a forced landing among the Germans.

As I turned away I could see that there were five columns of infantry, which indicated there would be an engagement on the front within the next 24 hours.

The CO had now identified a field near the village of Aspelaere, west of Brussels, which would serve as an advance landing ground, allowing our aircraft to be refuelled nearer to the area of operations. However, the next day I had just landed back from a sortie over the front lines and was walking towards the tent to be interrogated by the Army intelligence officers when the field was attacked by about 20 German bombers. They were bombing the main road from Brussels to Tournai to harass the refugees pouring out of Brussels to make their way westwards towards France, where they had hoped to find safety.

The bombers' main target appeared to be the crossroads at the corner of our field, though they may have noticed our three or four Lysanders standing near a small plantation about 300 yards away. I decided to seek refuge by running as fast as I could to the ditch at the edge of the field.

Chapter 5

As I threw myself into it, the last of a stick of bombs hit the edge. The blast covered me with earth, but I was very relieved to find I was unhurt. I didn't realise that my hearing in both ears had been seriously impaired.

The ground party, which included the Army intelligence officers, left Aspelaere the next day. I had been billeted in a house by a T-junction in the village, on one of the roads the withdrawing British forces were using along their route to the west. It was a very sharp corner and many of the Bren gun carriers had to reverse to negotiate it. Some of the vehicles towing field guns also had difficulty in getting round it, and all the noise meant that I had very little sleep.

However I was due to take off again at first light to do the dawn sortie over the front, so this made it easy for me to be up very early to start my walk to the airfield. Here I joined a long line of refugees who were walking out of the village, past the airfield and on to the main road, where they would turn right towards Tournai and the French frontier.

The pilots were briefed at Aspelaere by Army intelligence officers. Having completed our sorties, we landed back at Lille Ronchin. Aspelaere was left empty, except for one Lysander which was upside down in the middle of the field - one of the departing airmen set fire to it before leaving. The remainder of our sorties were now to be carried out from Lille Ronchin.

When we returned to Lille, the airfield was undamaged but the city was deserted, and we were billeted close to the airfield in houses which had been abandoned by their owners. Wing Commander Charles (he had been promoted) called a meeting of the six pilots at nine o'clock that night and warned us that we should be remaining in Lille as long as the Army needed our services. He pointed out that our aircraft comprised the last unit serving within the encircled British Expeditionary Force, and that we should be proud of the honour which had befallen us.

The next morning I was ordered to complete a dawn sortie over the front, which was now the line of the River Escaut east of Lille, only ten minutes' flying time away.

Our losses continued to mount, and before we left Lille we had lost 13 aircraft and crews - over half the Squadron.

We then flew to Clairmarais, near St Omer, landing at dusk, and spent the night there. On the way there, Pilot Officer Scott force-landed due to engine trouble and spent a night in a field with an Army unit. He had to clear his air intake, which had caused him partial engine failure.

At Clairmarais we had a sparse meal of sardines and hard biscuits with margarine. We were keen to get some sleep in the house near the wood. I used a sleeping bag belonging to Pilot Officer Tom Pierce, who had slept there two nights before. He must have left in a hurry and forgotten to take it with him.

The next day was May 25. At about 2 am the CO woke me and told me to accompany him, as there was some trouble with the men on guard. We walked across the airfield, where one of the airmen told us that a German pilot who had been shot down that afternoon had apparently climbed into the cockpit of a five-seater de Havilland Domine. As we were talking, a rifle shot rang out from the cover of the wood on the other side of the aircraft, and one of our men fired back at the flash.

The CO, who had not put on his belt and revolver, said to me "Give me your gun, take this torch and we'll check the aircraft." We crept the 60 or 70 yards to the aircraft and he whispered: "Flash your torch on to the door as you open it and I'll cover the German with my gun".

As I reached for the door it was opened from within by one of our own pilots, who had evidently been asleep inside the aircraft. "What the hell is going on?" he said. While the CO was explaining what had happened, we noticed the sound of petrol pouring from the aircraft's tank. One of the bullets from the two rifle shots had holed it. The aircraft had to be burned before the CO left the field.

We returned to our sleeping bags, but half an hour later the CO again woke me and ordered me to get the ground party to leave immediately. An Army despatch rider had arrived to warn us that while we were in the north part of the wood, German tanks were occupying the south side. We realised afterwards that they must have been Rommel's Panzers. The CO told us to board our aircraft, start up and keep the engines running. If there was any sign of the Germans moving on to the field, we should take off into the mist and darkness.

After we had been sitting in the aircraft for about 30 minutes, the CO told us to take off and fly to Dunkirk, where we might find petrol and ammunition so that we could continue to assist the Army. But when we got there, we found that no petrol was available.

Eventually the CO arrived by road and told us to fly over to Hawkinge, near Folkestone. We arrived there in time for breakfast, and found it full of fighter aircraft covering the evacuation.

From Hawkinge we were sent to RAF Detling, near Maidstone, where we were immediately given 24 hours' leave. When we returned, the six of us received orders to fly to RAF Ringway, near Manchester, where the Squadron was reforming and reorganising. The flight now included Gerry Scott, who had caught up with us at Detling.

The Squadron was reunited with its ground crews at Ringway. On arrival, we were billeted in various houses and enjoyed the comfort of clean sheets and pleasant bedrooms. I found myself in the home of a man who owned a cotton factory. It was large, with a very large and well-tended garden, and I was given a small room which belonged to one of the housemaids. I remember the owner complained that they were short of staff to assist in the house and garden because so many of their employees had been called up.

He had two sons who were still employed in the family business, and one of them seemed resentful at having an RAF pilot imposed on the household. Nevertheless they gave me breakfast for two or three mornings, and I was very grateful. On the first night I slept like a log and was very reluctant to get out of my warm bed.

Ringway would later evolve into the vastly larger and busier Manchester Airport, but back then it was the site of one of A V Roe's large factories and was developing a new heavy bomber, the Avro Manchester. It was driven by two propellers, each powered by two Rolls Royce Vulture engines mounted one above the other. These new aircraft did go into service squadrons, but there were many teething troubles. Manufacture was discontinued, and the aeroplane and wings were used to house four Rolls Royce Merlin engines. In this form it became the Lancaster bomber, the most successful aircraft of Bomber Command.

Our airmen were arriving at Ringway in ones and twos. They included the wireless operators who had been attached to the artillery regiments working with the BEF (British Expeditionary Force), who were among the last to be taken off the beaches. They had been relaying W/T messages from us to the troop or battery commanders in charge of the guns, translating them into verbal instructions so that the commanders knew exactly what was going on and where their shells were falling.

The wireless men spoke scathingly of the conduct of many of the Army units in their retreat from the line of the river Escaut back to Dunkirk. The airmen in turn had to suffer the taunts of many of the soldiers who wanted to know where the RAF had got to. We who had just returned from the battle area with our aircraft could well understand this, as we had seen no British fighters over the battle areas or the front line while we had been operating with the Army before our withdrawal on May 24.

Yet these same men spoke tremendously highly of the conduct of the Royal Navy. I remember talking to two of them who said "Thank God we have a Navy." It was marvellous the way the Navy men marshalled the Army, who sometimes appeared a bit of a rabble. The Naval officers in charge of the embarkation would threaten the soldiers, guns in hand, if they didn't quickly obey orders.

One of the operators said that the beaches were considered to be the safest place to wait to be picked up, because the impact of the German bombs was absorbed by the sand. He said one of his colleagues had been manning a Bren gun mounted on a makeshift post close to the edge of the sea. He had managed to score a direct hit on a Stuka which was dive-bombing the area.

Chapter 5

One of my first jobs at Ringway was to look after a Lysander which had been damaged by machine-gun fire. It was the aircraft Gerry Scott had flown when he had discovered German tanks on the southern edge of the forest of Clairmarais. One bullet had made a neat one-inch hole in one of the main struts which supported the port wing. I was told to take it for repair to the airfield at Eastleigh, where the Spitfires were being made.

When I arrived at Eastleigh and reported to the flying control office, an engineer from the factory told me they didn't repair Lysanders there. He told me he could not give me permission to take off again, because the strut could fail at any moment. Later he came back to say he had contacted the Squadron and had been told I should take the aircraft to the Westland Aircraft factory at Yeovil, where the Lysander was manufactured.

I flew to Yeovil with another pilot, who was also flying a damaged Lysander, and we left our aircraft in the hands of one of the ground engineers there. When we reported back a few days later to collect our repaired aircraft, my overalls had been stolen from the map case. Fortunately we had removed our Squadron flying badges from the breast pockets.

After about ten days at Ringway we were ordered to fly to RAF Linton-on-Ouse, a large bomber airfield a few miles north of York. There the Squadron was given the use of about a quarter of a hangar and two offices built into the side of the hangar. This gave us the first opportunity in many months to work on our aircraft under cover.

It also enabled the pilots to continue with their training. We now had with us a number of new pilots who had been hurriedly trained in the UK before being sent to France, and many of them had not been with us long enough to undertake any operations before we returned to the UK. So there were a number who needed further air experience.

We shared the station at Linton-on-Ouse with two heavy bomber squadrons equipped with the Whitley Bombers which were engaged every night in attacking Germany. Until the Battle of France they had been allowed to drop only pamphlets over Germany, for fear of provoking the Germans into dropping bombs on England.

We remained at Linton for about a month. One night we learned that an enemy pilot had spotted the night-flying lights which we had placed along the runway. I and many other Lysander pilots were told to land. Unfortunately one of our pilots parked his aircraft on the approach to the runway. After we had all landed, a Whitley bomber signalled that it had suspected engine trouble and was returning to base. The pilot, a Squadron Leader, made a perfect very low approach – straight towards the parked Lysander.

I was standing by the second flare when the Whitley struck the Lysander. The whole lot slithered about a hundred yards along the runway and burst into flames. As the bomber came to rest, we could see figures running from the wreckage, their flying clothes ablaze. They had no idea what their plane had hit.

I ran as hard as I could towards the runway, only to be stopped by one of the fleeing crew, who was very badly shaken. He told me not to go any nearer to the aircraft, because it still had a full bomb load aboard. Just then I saw a huge blaze erupt in the body of the aircraft, followed by a spectacular explosion as the first of the bombs went off.

I ran as fast as I could the other way, hoping that all the crew had escaped. Whether they had or not, there was no chance of any of us entering that inferno to see if we could rescue them.

Clearly the German bomber was still up there, because as the bombs continued to go off one after another, he dropped a parachute flare. The whole place was lit up as if by daylight, and it stayed that way for something like four minutes. You could have read a newspaper by it. At last the runway returned to darkness and the German bomber flew off, without, I think, dropping any bombs.

A week or two after arriving at Linton I received a letter from the Chief of the Air Staff telling me I had been awarded the DFC (Distinguished

Flying Cross) for gallantry and devotion to duty during the campaign in France. Drewitt, my air gunner, was awarded a DFM (Distinguished Flying Medal), which was richly deserved. He had been a great help to me during our operational flights.

It was soon clear that space at Linton-on-Ouse was severely limited. More heavy bombers were coming on to the station for operational flights over Germany, so we were ordered to move to a small civil airport at Clifton on the outskirts of York, the home of the York flying club. It was a small airfield with few facilities except a couple of Nissen huts and wooden huts which housed the airmen and NCOs.

Most of the officers were billeted in houses in the vicinity, so we all had comfortable beds within easy walking distance of the airfield. The sergeants were accommodated in a makeshift but comfortable building, and there was a large dining room which would serve as our mess. It was a very pleasant place to be stationed, within walking distance of the centre of York and with delightful wooded countryside to the north.

While we were at Linton I received an invitation to go to Buckingham Palace to receive my DFC from His Majesty King George VI. I arranged to meet my mother and sister Joan at Paddington so that they could accompany me to the Palace. We were shown to our seats in a large reception room, where there was a small orchestra playing quietly. There were a lot of people there who had won their awards during the Dunkirk evacuation, and His Majesty was pinning medals on their chests one by one.

The King shook my hand (I remember being told not to return the handshake too tightly). My citation read: "Early on the morning of 13th May, this officer was on reconnaissance in the neighbourhood of Tirlemont. Under heavy fire he descended to 50 feet to ascertain the nationality of the hostile troops. Pilot Officer Malins has distinguished himself on several occasions by his excellent reconnaissance over the enemy."

It was a wonderfully proud moment for all of us.

Chapter 6

Coastal defence and reconnaissance
1940-41

Just before we left our base at Linton-on-Ouse, Wing Commander Charles called me into his office and told me that Flight Lieutenant Wally Barton had been granted compassionate leave to return to Canada because of a family bereavement. It was unlikely that he would return to the Squadron because he might be required to take up a post in the new Empire Flying Training Scheme which was now being started for countries such as Canada, Rhodesia and America.

Charles told me he had been impressed with my operational flying during the fortnight of the Battle for France, especially the hectic three days before we had left for England. He had therefore recommended to Group HQ that I be appointed Flight Commander and promoted to the rank of acting Flying Officer, pending a further promotion to the acting rank of Flight Lieutenant. He thought they might have a substantive Flight Lieutenant already in mind to take over B Flight, but he would do his best to ensure that my appointment as Flight Commander was confirmed by Group HQ. This would mean that after three months as an acting Flying Officer I would be eligible for promotion to acting Flight Lieutenant.

He said he had every confidence in me, and his last words before I left the office were "Don't let me down". I like to think I didn't.

With the evacuation of the British forces from Dunkirk, there was a real danger that the south east would be invaded by the German forces if they could quickly assemble barges or assault craft to bring their troops the 20 miles or so across the Channel. All our training was now directed towards making sure that enemy forces were not attempting to reconnoitre the beaches or make a landing.

Chapter 6

We covered the east coast from the Wash to Berwick-upon-Tweed, from early dawn through till dusk. We would fly 15-20 miles off the coast, so that we could give an hour or two's warning of any shipping that might be moving towards our invasion beaches.

I was told by Wing Commander Charles that in the event of invasion we would spray the beaches with mustard gas. The combination of gas on top of a thickly-sown minefield would, he thought, seriously impede even the most determined assault troops. The code for this was Smoke Curtain Installation (SCI), which appears many times in my log book. Cylinders or barrels of mustard gas were brought to the airfields and stored in the B Flight area of the airfield, the rather more remote area on the eastern side which was well clear of housing. The cylinders were stored in the open, the topsoil having been removed to a depth of about six inches to contain any leaks.

The armament personnel had to be instructed in the care, storage and loading of the gas into the canisters, which would be carried on the stub wings of the Lysander aircraft. The gas would be released from the containers by an electrical device designed to fracture a bung in the base of the container, allowing it to flow at a pre-determined rate and form a fine spray.

We trained for this by spraying foot-square targets with a liquid which had the same properties as the mustard gas. We had to allow for the direction and speed of the wind to release the spray at the right moment.

Another part of our training involved firing our front guns at a 10 ft square target placed at the northern edge of the airfield. We approached the target from the south over a built-up area, so if the pilot opened fire a little too soon the shell cases and metallic parts of the ammunition belt fell on to the houses. We had to carry out this practice at first light so as not to disturb the residents. One of the local doctors, who was acting as our Squadron doctor at the time, told us that nine months later there was a significant increase in the birth rate in that part of York. He could only put it down to the fact that the rattle of our machine-gun fire at first light had roused many couples from their sleep.

We continued to support the units that formed the Northern Command of the British Army, and there was no respite. The local Home Guard proved to be an extremely efficient organisation. It was commanded by a farmer, Mr Crawford, who had been a captain in the Infantry in WW1. He was an excellent soldier and would have reached a senior position in the Army had he remained there.

I recall attending one of his conferences before an exercise which involved the Home Guard and hearing him say: "We don't want concrete buildings erected in this part of the country. We saw in France that concrete pill boxes don't stop the Germans. If we have to meet any parachutists we will use the ditches and the woods and houses, where we can move quickly. It'll be a case of fire and move". He was a remarkable man, and he had the right idea about how the area should be defended.

Flying accidents still occurred. One new pilot with an above-average assessment from his flying school flew his aircraft straight into the ground while attacking a 10 ft sq target. I was standing in the CO's office facing the airfield and saw the whole thing. He failed to pull out in time, and I watched the aircraft breaking up as it slid nose first along the ground. The air gunner, who was enjoying what he thought was simply an interesting flight, got away with a few bruises, but the pilot was killed.

Another pilot crashed his aircraft into a doctor's garden as he was returning home in near-darkness. He was retained as the CO's personal assistant and as a Liaison Officer with Northern Command HQ in York, until he crashed the CO's Humber at 80 mph. He escaped with a broken nose, but this time the CO did not object to his posting to India.

We undertook intensive training in night flying, so that we could land on the airfield comfortably by the light of a half moon and without ground lights. We managed this easily enough, particularly when we were able to take advantage of the full moon, and many of us were soon able to make good landings in semi-darkness.

Chapter 6

The reason for this training was that the powers that be had decided that the Lysanders were to be used to take agents into France and land them in specified fields where French reception committees would be waiting. We were also able to bring back agents carrying vital information about German formations in the area. When I heard that Gordon Scotter, a pilot officer in No.2 Squadron who had been my co-pilot at the flying training school in Sealand, had already carried out such a flight, I decided to go to his base in Sawbridgeworth to find out if it was true.

I found that Gordon had in fact completed two successful pickups. But this cloak-and-dagger work required great concentration and willpower, and both flights had been much more difficult than Gordon had anticipated. He had had some trouble locating the right field, and the Frenchmen, waiting on the ground with torches to indicate where he should land, had been slow to respond to his flashing light. Those flights had taken 5_ to 6 hours, so he had been quite exhausted when he returned back to England. However, they had produced vital information, so Gordon had helped to pave the way for a new type of operation which would gather strength over the next months and years.

Later on in the war I met up with John Nesbitt Dufour, who had been flying agents back into France. He did extraordinarily well. On one occasion his aircraft got bogged down and he couldn't take off. He had to set fire to it and then tell the French Resistance to get him to Spain so that he could get back to England that way.

Between June and September 1940 we were joined by fresh crews to replace the men we had lost in France in May. Our 13 losses over just 16 days represented well over half the Squadron.

Sadly, we then had a series of unfortunate accidents. One pilot decided to fly over to Scarborough and 'beat up' his family's home, which was near the seafront on the outskirts of the town. He flew into a severe downdraft near the cliff edge and crashed into the house next to his parents'. Both he and his air gunner were killed.

Chapter 6

Another young pilot who had joined the wing only a few weeks earlier got lost in bad weather over Ilkley Moor; he too crashed and was killed.

Despite this, our young airmen were keen to take advantage of any opportunity to fly in the rear cockpit. Many of them harboured ideas that they might one day be able to qualify as aircrew, preferably as pilots, so this was an opportunity to get in some air experience, if only as a passenger.

At York we continued with our coastal reconnaissance flights at dawn and again in the evening. We dropped live bombs on the bombing range at Fylingdales on the Yorkshire moors, and continued with our gas spraying training.

One young pilot who joined us that summer was Pilot Officer Peter Vaughan-Fowler. He had a most successful tour flying agents into France with the Lysander flight and obtained a DSO and two DFCs. Eventually he became Deputy Captain of the Queen's Flight.

Soon after the war had ended Vaughan-Fowler, who by then had a family of four strapping boys and four delightful girls, was given a large house at Bicester airfield, so we were able to renew our acquaintance. On retirement he took a house in Oxford, where his widow still lives. We remain in contact with one of his grandchildren, who attends the Oxford High School for Girls, along with my granddaughters Holly and Annabel.

Five or six pilots had joined the Squadron a few days before the blitz started on May 10 in France. One of them, Pilot Officer MacDonald, suffered an engine failure while taking off from Lille-Ronchin and had to make a forced landing among the factories and workers' housing which surrounded the airfield. He was unable to find a large enough space for a safe landing and crashed into one of the houses, sustaining serious injuries. He was put on to one of the last hospital trains leaving Lille for Boulogne and reached England safely, where he made a full recovery. He was able to return to the Squadron that autumn.

Another of the new pilots, Pilot Officer Tony Fegen, crashed with engine failure while taking off from a small airfield near Lille Ronchin. He was put on the last hospital train from Lille to Boulogne and reached England safely, where he too recuperated and rejoined the Squadron towards the end of 1940.

Tony Fegen was the nephew of Captain Fegen, the Commander of the armed merchant ship Jervis Bay. In the late autumn of 1940 the Jervis Bay was escorting a convoy heading for England from America when Captain Fegen received intelligence concerning the movements of a German battleship heading towards his convoy. He ordered the convoy to scatter and told the Jervis Bay, armed with a single gun, to steer towards the battleship to engage it. Unfortunately the ship was quickly blown out of the sea and lost. Only 65 of the 255 men on board were rescued.

That autumn, Tony Fegen received a letter from his uncle. It must have been handed to an escorting destroyer before the Jervis Bay was sunk. In it was a cheque for £5 for his birthday and a note which said that so far they were having a pleasant voyage, but it looked as if they might soon be very busy; it appeared to be a coded message of warning.

When Tony told us of this in the mess, the Adjutant, Flight Lieutenant Bencher, offered to give him a fiver for the cheque. He said he would like to keep it as a reminder of Tony's uncle's gallantry. This Tony did. I often wonder what happened to the cheque and the letter, both of which would be of great historical interest.

In mid-December 1940 I developed a severe throat infection and was admitted to York Military Hospital. The medical attention was first class and the food adequate. The Colonel in charge of the hospital spoke with a pronounced Irish accent. On learning that I was an RAF pilot, he said to the matron: "We must get these RAF chaps back to their squadrons as soon as possible. Give this man a bottle of Guinness with his lunch." From then on I had a Guinness every day.

Chapter 6

I was discharged from hospital just before Christmas, in time to take part in the Christmas festivities. On New Year's Eve we had a rather special celebration in the Station Hotel in York, where we gathered to say goodbye to Guy Charles. He had been given notice that he would be posted overseas within a couple of weeks. He told us that he had been awarded an OBE, as had all the other squadron commanders who had taken part in the battle for France. At the same time, almost all those who had commanded squadrons during the Battle of Britain had been awarded the Distinguished Service Order (DSO).

It was a well deserved award. Wing Commander Charles was a much respected CO, and it was with great regret that a couple of years later we heard that he had been shot down and killed while testing a Hurricane in the Canal Zone in Egypt.

In January 1941 it was agreed that the Army Co-operation Squadrons should be equipped with fighter aircraft when available, to give them a chance of surviving over the front line if they were intercepted by enemy fighters. We were told that we would probably get the Curtis Tomahawk, which had a performance about equal to or slightly better than a Hurricane. After the fall of France, ships carrying Tomahawks there had been diverted to Liverpool, where the aeroplanes were assembled on Speke Airfield. One, two or sometimes even three aircraft were then allocated to the existing Army Co-operation Squadrons.

The Tomahawk soon earned a doubtful reputation. One of the first squadrons equipped with them was No.400 Canadian Squadron, which suffered a number of accidents when the aircraft swung badly either on landing or take-off. I found no difficulty in flying the Tomahawk however; it simply needed a little bit of care in taking off and landing to counteract the swing.

Chapter 7

Training and surveillance
1941-42

1941 was to prove relatively uneventful for our Squadron. We stayed at York for the whole year, except for two periods of attachment to the Armament Training Camp at Westonzoyland in Somerset. We carried on our normal training: reporting on the movement of British troops during the Brigade and Divisional exercises, and photographing defences being built along river lines or other natural obstacles. Our brief was generally to locate military formations on the ground and to photograph their defensive positions to see if they had been adequately camouflaged.

One of my most interesting jobs that year was demonstrating gas-spraying to trainees at the Northern Command Gas School up in the Lake District. It was housed in buildings located on a triangular spit of land which jutted into Ullswater from the western bank. The Army Gas School took groups of officers from all the units in Northern Command. During their short stay there they would be exposed to gas spray under field conditions.

The hills at the southern end of Lake Ullswater were 2000 feet high, so this was a mission that could only be undertaken in good weather by experienced pilots. When you reached the southern end of the lake you had to dive steeply at the same angle as the slope of the mountain, then level out 50 feet above the water and about a quarter of a mile from the spit of land where the school was based. As you skimmed overhead you sprayed simulated gas at the Army personnel who were on the course, and they had to learn to take evasive action.

We helped artillery regiments training on the ranges in Northumberland. We would notify the gunners by R/T (speech, rather than morse code) where their shells were falling in relation to the target, and we were soon able to issue instructions to the gunners to help them improve their accuracy.

We had plenty of time for games that summer. There was cricket and tennis, and I'm happy to report that the Squadron cricket team, of which I was a member, won the local cricket league. It's odd to think that a collection of airmen could win a cricket league in Yorkshire, the home of the best cricketers in England.

We went further the following spring when we won a silver challenge cup in the football league, after a final played at York City Football Ground. I protested that my soccer skills were rusty, but the Corporal in charge of cricket persuaded me to play outside left. I don't think my contribution made much difference, but we did win the cup.

In the late summer of 1941 I was able to take a few days' leave to return home and give a hand with our small harvest. Daphne and I had remained in close contact, and I now decided it was time to propose.

I went into the kitchen at Bignell Farm, where Mr Dickins was having his supper, and asked his permission to marry Daphne. "She's a very precious member of the family" he said. He went on a bit, but in the end he said "All right then". I remember spending £25 on her engagement ring, which we chose together. We made plans to get married the following year, 1942, on March 21.

In early 1942 a new plane came along, the North American-made Mustang. We had to fly up to Speke Airfield near Liverpool to collect four of them, so I took four pilots in a Fairey Battle and they flew the new aircraft back to York.

We spent the next few weeks getting used to them. The Mustang was one of the fastest fighters in England at up to about 5000 feet, where it was much faster than the Hurricane and slightly faster than the Spitfire Mark II. Most of the pilots found it a fairly easy aircraft to fly and were very comfortable with it, and there were no accidents or burst tyres. It had no

My grandfather, William Malins, grandmother, Annie Cecilia (centre), and their children: Nellie, William Vernon (my father) and Dora.

Lords Farm around 1903, showing the thatched roof that burned so readily.

My grandparents (William and Annie Cecilia) and my sister Marjorie outside Lords Farm in the four-wheeler (the "poor man's Phaeton") around 1910.

Lords Farm around 1910. Grandpa Malins can just be seen near the back door, while Aunt Dora feeds the chickens.

My grandparents with the horses at the back of Lords Farm around 1910. The water tower which was so unfortunately empty on the day of the fire is visible in the background.

Haymaking in Oxford Road field (rented by Grandpa Malins) around 1912. Second and third from the left in the cart are Will Jeacock and Harry Cripps. Seated on their left, with hat and moustache, is my father.

As a baby in 1915 with my three big sisters, Marjorie, Joan and Nellie.

Posing with a horsewhip at the age of three or four, at
James & Son photographers in Bicester.

Me with my arm around Chetwode, the cow I milked every afternoon, around 1926.

On my pony Flossie, with my sister Marjorie holding her (1928)

My mother in the garden at Lords Farm in 1930 (photo by Harris Morgan)

On holiday in Jersey in 1937 with my friend Albert Buckle

Me (second from left, middle row) with the Oxford Nomads Rugby Club team in 1938.
Bob Deeley was the captain (seated with the ball), and Emrys Watkins is to his left.

This photo was used in a 1938 advertisement for de Havilland Gipsy engines in Flight magazine. I'm third on the left, holding map, talking to Peter West. Behind Peter, Gordon Scotter is talking to Doug Bagnell.

In front of a Hawker Audax at RAF Sealand, 1938

With B Flight at Lille Ronchin, May 1940. My Air Gunner, L A C Drewitt, is rear left, I'm second left on the front row.

My flying log-book with the DFC citation I keep inside it

With Gerry Scott at Clifton, York, in August 1940. Our DFCs had already been sewn on to our jackets, although we did not receive the medals until later. When I got my jacket back, the seamstress had put a note inside saying "Congratulations. We love you! We're proud of you"

At Buckingham Palace to receive my DFC in September 1940, with Joan and my mother.

Portrait by Ramsey & Muspratt of Oxford, taken while I was on leave in December 1940 at the request of my mother, in case they never saw me again.

With a Lysander at Clifton, 1941 – you can see the mustard gas container
fitted ready for gas spray training.

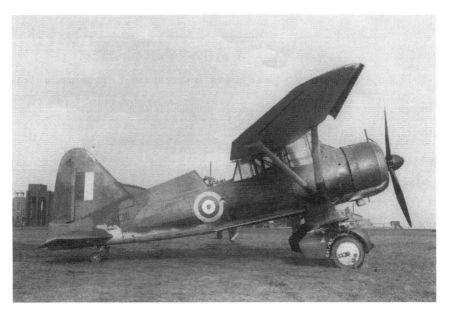

A Lysander at RAF Clifton

My Alvis Crested Eagle, bought for £5 because it needed repairs, then sold for £70 in 1942 to help pay for our wedding.

Our wedding day, March 21 1942

The newly-weds

In the cockpit of a Mustang Mk I, April 1943

Daphne with our firstborn, Anita, aged 3 months (1943)

On arrival in Mönchengladbach, Germany, March 1945

At Twente Enschede, Holland, around the time the war ended, with Group Captain Anderson (centre) and Pilot Officer Jack Grimwood.

SS guards captured at Belsen in Celle prison, April 1945

The courtroom at Lüneburg where the guards were tried in the autumn of 1945. Eleven of the 30 were sentenced to hang.

A flypast we staged as a farewell to General Crerar, General Officer Commanding,
Canadian Army, at the end of May 1945 – I'm in the lead Spitfire.

My gliding certificate and green ticket

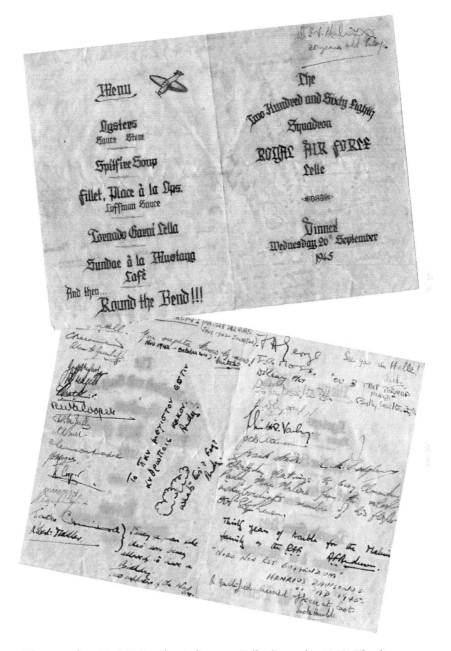

The menu from No.268 Squadron's dinner at Celle, September 1945. The dinner was held on my 30th birthday and everyone signed it for me. "Round the Bend" was the name we gave to the cellar bar.

Hunting wild boar in the Harz mountains, 1945

Skiing near Volkenrode, while I was commanding the research station there (I'm in the centre of group shot)

An aerial view of Volkenrode, showing a hangar and part of the airfield

At the gliding club at RAF Salzgitter, 1946

My Sudanese trader, Moustafa Farahat, and his family. He had two wives and six sons.

In front of the Taj Mahal, 1947

Lords Farm, 1946 - my sister Joan on the tractor, Tony Butt on the mowing
machine and Bert Phipps standing

Me (on the reaper-binder) and my father (on the tractor) in Lambourne's Ground, 1955.

My son John and my father by the old cowshed at Lords Farm, 1953.

With a young pedigree Guernsey bull in the rickyard at Lords Farm, 1955.

My youngest daughter, Jennifer, in the garden at Lords Farm, 1960.

My sons Tim (second left) and John (right) at Hawkwell Farm
with George Davies and David Spencer, 1978.

From left: my daughter Anita, granddaughters Jessica, Catherine, and Amanda, grandson
Mark and son Tim with a calf named Popstar born in 1981, the biggest we've ever had.

With my sisters Joan, Marjorie and Nellie, 1985

Making my speech at our 50th wedding anniversary party in 1992,
with Daphne and life-long friend Gerry Scott.

With my granddaughters Holly (left) and Sophie.

(From left) my grandson Mark and son Tim with Dickie and Lennie Allen,
who are sitting on a round silage bale wrapper (1995)

Lords Farm as it is today, one storey less than it was before the fire.

A 1997 visit to 133 Rue de Douai, Lille Ronchin, where I was billeted in
November 1939, with the daughter of airman George Wood, who was in France with
me in 1940 and my daughter Marijoy (centre).

With Daphne, cutting our cake at our 60th wedding anniversary party in March 2002.

Inspecting the maize crop, 2009

Christmas Day 2009

obvious vices, and would prove to be the ideal fighter-type aircraft for reconnaissance purposes.

In silhouette, the aircraft looked a little like the Bf 109, so I was detailed to take the aircraft to a number of fighter stations in the north of England to let them have a good look at it, to make sure it wouldn't be mistaken for an enemy aircraft and shot down by our own side.

On 19th March 1942, two days before I was due to marry Daphne, I had to fly some Major Generals from York to Farnborough. When I dropped them off the weather had closed in and I was refused permission to take off back to York. Luckily, my CO arranged for the aircraft to be picked up so that I could make my way to Bicester by train in order to get there in time for our wedding two days later.

We got married in Chesterton parish church, where Daphne had been a regular communicant. It was a spring day and we had a modest ceremony with family and a few friends present. Gerry Scott was my best man, and a couple of other members of the Squadron travelled down from York.

During the war it was strictly forbidden to ring church bells – they were only to be rung when invasion was imminent. However one of our RAF guests managed to put the wind up Daphne and her parents by threatening to ring the bells at the end of the service.

The report on our wedding in the local newspaper noted: "The interior of the church presented a pleasing appearance, Mrs Anderson and Mrs P F White having carried out effective decorations with daffodils, evergreens, and pot flowers, the last-named kindly lent by Mrs How... The bride, given away by her father, was attired in a frock and coatee of pastel blue, with navy blue accessories, and her bouquet was of crimson roses." The reception was held at Daphne's parents' farm, Bignell Park Farm, Chesterton, and about 80 people were there.

After a week's honeymoon in Paignton, Daphne came back to York with me. We lived in a hotel there for a week before finding digs with a pleasant couple who lived close to the airfield. Daphne fitted very easily into squadron life and became a popular member of our little officers' mess.

In early July 1942 I was told I was being posted to No.268 Reconnaissance Squadron, which was stationed at Snailwell, near Newmarket. This was a Squadron Leader posting, so it meant promotion and a considerable rise in my service pay. Since I would need time to find accommodation for Daphne, we travelled down by train to Peterborough and Daphne returned to Bicester while I went on to my new base.

The CO, Wing Commander Anderson DFC, wasn't there when I arrived, so I was met by one of the Air Liaison Officers, an Army officer acting as an Air Intelligence Liaison Officer. I was told that they were engaged in an exercise with the Army and asked if I would like to do the early morning sortie. I thought I'd better show some keenness, so I said I'd be glad to and he promised I would be woken at 4.30 am.

The next morning I was duly awoken by one of the officer's servants, who brought me a cup of tea, and taken to the airfield. Here I was briefed to search for the field artillery batteries which were camouflaged, effectively they hoped, in various parts of the training area, near Thetford in the neighbouring county of Norfolk.

I took off on a beautiful bright sunny morning, the sun just above the horizon. I managed to locate most of the guns. After the sortie, which lasted about two hours, I arrived back at the station, and as I was being debriefed Wing Commander Anderson walked in. This was the first time I'd met my new CO, and he greeted me warmly. He was obviously held in high regard by the other officers, and indeed he proved to be one of the finest officers I had met.

He had been seconded to the Royal Air Force from the Army about five years previously and had joined the Warwickshire Regiment on leaving the Army college at Woolwich. He had then served in the Royal Warwickshire Regiment in Egypt, commanded by Lieutenant Colonel

Montgomery. Wing Commander Anderson had earned his DFC also during the Battle for France, in his case flying Hawker Hector light bombers in diving bombing attacks in support of the besieged British troops at Calais.

Wing Commander Anderson asked me to join him in his office, where he told me a little about No.268 Squadron and its operational role. He told me they had already been engaged on shipping reconnaissances along the Dutch coast from the Hook of Holland up to the German islands. Their job was to report any German shipping, the direction it was heading, the size of the merchantmen and details of any small battleships or destroyers escorting it. We would then race back the hundred miles or so across the North Sea and report what we had seen.

If the target was considered big enough - one or more large merchant ships – Beaufighters and the Mosquitoes of Coastal Command would be briefed to attack it with bombs and rockets. It was up to our Squadron to keep the area covered by making frequent sorties along the coast throughout the day. When we were not required for this reconnaissance, we could undertake low-level sorties into Holland to attack military targets.

On these flights there was always the risk of being intercepted by German fighters stationed at airfields up the channel coast through Belgium and Holland and into northern Germany. I found that the best way to avoid their attention was to cross the North Sea at low level, dropping to the lowest possible safe level as we approached the Dutch coast. This way we would not be picked up by German radar. After reaching the coast we would accelerate almost to maximum speed towards the German coast. If we came from the other direction, we would sometimes start from the German islands and move south to Belgium and then turn for home across the North Sea.

Flying fast made it difficult for aircraft coming from behind to catch up with us. The danger was that aircraft would be sent from airfields slightly ahead of us, allowing the Germans to attack us head on or come round behind with a diving turn and start a dogfight.

The larger merchantmen were often protected by small ships carrying a host of anti-aircraft guns of all calibres. However, finding them, reporting their headings and speed and estimating the number of escorting anti aircraft ships was a relatively safe job. We operated our aircraft in twos, sometimes fours. Occasionally, if a special operation was ordered, as many as eight would take part. We would also look for ships towing barrage balloons, which were a threat to low-flying aircraft attacking them.

Pilots flying over land would take pot shots at any transport on the Dutch roads which appeared to be German. It was sometimes difficult to know if you were firing at part of a military convoy or a farmer, because the German infantry divisions were still using horses. The poor Dutch farmers had to produce hay and straw, oats and other fodder to feed the horses of the occupying army.

On October 21 1942 my number two and I were ordered to carry out a reconnaissance over Holland, but not to penetrate too far unless there was ample cloud cover to hide in. After a few miles I decided to withdraw and turned steeply and at very low level. It so happened that we were turning above a football match, where they stopped playing to wave at us flying above them at only 40 feet. I was afraid I might puncture their football with my propeller.

On the way out we attacked both the gas holder at Katwijk aan Zee and a very large cement mixer which the Germans were using to build their fortifications along the Dutch coast.

Life in Newmarket was very comfortable. The officers' mess there had been the premises of the Calcutta Club, which was used by many racehorse trainers and owners. It provided fine accommodation, with splendid bedrooms and a very nice lawn on which we could play bowls. I found a very pleasant bed-and-breakfast in Newmarket for myself and Daphne, and she soon joined me there.

I used a bicycle to get from there to the airfield, and when Daphne got a job at Barclays Bank in Newmarket she got one of her own to enable her to cycle into town.

Wing Commander Anderson left the Squadron that November for a three-month course at Staff College. He was replaced by Wing Commander Peter Dudgeon, an old Etonian who arrived at the Squadron in a Rolls Royce. He was not of the same calibre as Anderson and flew very few, if any, operational sorties, but he was a jovial character and the pilots in the squadron found him a reasonable CO.

Wing Commander Dudgeon was in turn replaced in February 1943 by Wing Commander Larry Ling, who had seen three or four years' service in the Middle East. Ling had had great experience in dealing with the people of that region, both the friendly ones and those who were not so friendly. In April and May 1941 he had been one of the instructors based at the RAF airfield at Habbaniya, which had come under attack from rebel Iraqi troops under the control of Rashid Ali, supported by a number of Luftwaffe aircraft flying in Iraqi colours. As it was a training base, all the RAF had to defend it were hastily-armed and converted training types, supported by other RAF aircraft which were eventually flown in to help put down the rebellion. It was stopped only by the arrival of a relief column from Palestine.

Ling was six feet three inches tall and powerfully built, so he had great difficulty fitting into the little cockpit of a Mustang. In fact, the Squadron engineer officer produced a special bulged top section to the cockpit hood for his Mustang to allow him a little more headroom.

Like Wing Commander Dudgeon, Larry Ling carried out few operational sorties. He had had the indignity of being shot through both buttocks by enemy machine gun fire while conducting dive bombing attacks using a Hawker Audax.

By chance Tony Dudgeon, the brother of Wing Commander Peter Dudgeon, was one of the other senior pilots at Habbaniya and had flown alongside Ling.

Chapter 7

A few months after my arrival at No.268 Squadron we were joined by two exceptional pilots, Tony Bird and Tony Bethell. Both had wanted to be fighter pilots, but they enjoyed their new posting and could fly the Mustangs as well as anybody. Tony Bethell shot down two German aircraft during a sortie into Holland, but was himself shot down on his next outing while crossing the coast at low level. After landing wheels up with the nose of his aircraft perched on the edge of a wide dyke, he was captured and eventually taken to Stalag Luft III, then the main prison for British airmen.

In March 1944 Tony Bethell became involved in the notorious Great Escape, when 76 officers escaped from Stalag Luft III through tunnels driven under the fence of the prison camp. Since he had been one of the workers in the tunnel, he was one of the first to be allowed to escape.

Nearly all the escapees were recaptured and, on the orders of a furious Hitler, 50 of them were shot in cold blood, one of the worst atrocities of the war. Tony and a companion were among the lucky ones. They were caught after being on the run for four or five days, but spared. They were returned to the camp and stayed there until they were liberated at the end of the war. When by chance I met Tony after the war, he told me he thought that they had escaped death because they looked like Germans; they were both tall, fit young men with fair hair.

Tony Bird was considered to be an even better pilot than Tony Bethell. He knew how to fly the Mustang to its limits. He seemed indestructible and I thought he would survive the war, but it was not to be. Having obtained a DFC and Bar with our Squadron, he volunteered for a Mustang Mk.III Squadron which was engaged on long-range escort duties with Mosquitoes which were attacking targets in Denmark. On his last sortie the formation was attacked head on by a single enemy fighter. Tony kept on firing at the German, and the German kept on firing at him. Each was as brave as the other, and neither would give way. Their aircraft crashed head on and both men were killed instantly. The aircraft fell within 100 metres of each other, and it seems the Danes buried both pilots in the same cemetery.

On December 7 1942 I had been ordered to lead eight aircraft in an operation over northern Holland as a diversion for some light bombers from 2 Group which had been ordered to bomb the Philips works at Eindhoven. We crossed the coast safely south of Denhelder, but immediately after crossing I realised my aircraft must have been hit in the tail. It began to fly nose-heavy and I had to hold full throttle and keep the control column back almost against my seat to maintain height. Any reduction in speed allowed the nose to start dropping, so I was forced to leave the Squadron and turn north to come out over the North Sea between two Dutch islands.

Just before Christmas I was taken ill with jaundice and taken to White Lodge hospital in Newmarket, which was housed in the old workhouse. After eight or 10 days on a fat-free diet and no alcohol, I was allowed to return to the Squadron. There was no point in Daphne spending Christmas on her own, so she went back to her family in Oxfordshire.

In April 1943, while I was still at Newmarket, I had a telephone call to let me know that Daphne had given birth to our first child. As soon as he heard the news, my CO, Peter Dudgeon, suggested I take one of the aircraft and fly to Bicester to see my firstborn, which I was delighted to do. We decided to call her Anita.

In all, life was very comfortable. But it was not long before I was to leave the shores of the UK far behind.

Chapter 8

The invasion of Sicily
1943

In May 1943 we heard that Army Cooperation Command was to be disbanded, to be replaced by the 2nd Tactical Air Force. This would constitute the air arm of the invasion forces which were to re-enter Europe in 1944. As 35 Reconnaissance Wing, we would be part of the newly-formed 84 Group working with the Canadian Army. The Canadian Reconnaissance Wing, consisting of three Canadian squadrons and one English squadron, would provide co-operation and reconnaissance for the British Second Army.

This meant moving to a suitable location in the south, where we could provide all the forms of reconnaissance necessary before the invasion took place. The whole coast from the Cherbourg peninsula to the Dutch frontier was to be photographed repeatedly, both from the sea and from the land, using low-flying aircraft. The photographs would provide a record of how far the German defences were progressing and where their anti-aircraft guns and other defensive armaments were sited.

Our new base was RAF Odiham in Hampshire, the location of my first posting. I led the Squadron there and we flew in in tight formation to let them know that No.268 Squadron had arrived. However, after reporting to the control tower and then to the officers' mess, I was told I had been posted to a 'planning cell', based in Norfolk House in St James' Square.

On reporting to Norfolk House three days later I was taken into a map room, where I was briefed on the preparations and planning for one of the major events of the war - the invasion of Sicily. The First Canadian Infantry Division, which was still training in Scotland, would be taking part. If everything went according to plan we would be going in on July 10.

I was astounded to be trusted with such vital and sensitive information. Naturally we were warned that we must on no account ever breathe a word of it to anyone.

I returned that evening to collect my belongings from Odiham. At breakfast the next morning, I was joined on the opposite side of the table by Tony Bird, who looked up at me and asked if I had had a good time in London. "What's the date for the invasion of Sicily?" he asked. He had known from the Adjutant that I must have been selected for this operation, because of the courses I had done. I had to brush aside his question.

I had been due to take ten days' leave, which I had hoped to use to get home to help with the haymaking. Instead I had to travel to Scotland to meet some of the Canadians who would be going to Sicily. I went up with Wing Commander Abrahams, who had been on the planning staff at Norfolk House for some months and was a very capable and likeable officer. He would be the senior officer on board the headquarters ship, HMS *Hilary*.

The *Hilary* was a converted merchantman operated by the Booth Shipping Line. She dealt mainly with freight from South America, so her usual route was the 2000-mile run up the Amazon to Manaos. There were a few spare cabins for passengers.

We did some training with the Canadians and prepared their vehicles for landing through the surf, which was known as 'waterproofing'. After a few days we had loaded all 12 of the ships in the convoy and were ready to set off. We sailed on June 28, 1943.

I had been unable to tell my wife or my parents where we were going or on what job I had been posted. All I could tell Daphne was that it wasn't a flying job, and that she might not hear from me for two or three months. As a staff officer, at least I was now relatively safe.

On reaching the mouth of Mersey and heading out into the Irish Sea, the convoy formed into three columns. As we rounded the north of Ireland we were told we would soon see the *Queen Mary*, approaching at full speed. She would be passing our convoy about a mile to the rear. She came into sight within a few minutes, travelling very fast and making a huge bow wave. It was a most encouraging sight, particularly as we knew she carried thousands of American soldiers who would be trained in England for the tremendous task of invading northern Europe.

To evade German long-range aircraft operating from bases in the west of France, our convoy steered a course which took them within a few miles of the Azores. It soon became very warm and the sea was calm, so it began to feel almost like a holiday.

Each morning we had training sessions in the operations room which had been built into the bowels of the ship, a smaller version of the Fighter Command operations room. Our afternoons were free, so we could stroll about the deck. All we had to do was keep out of the way of the Canadian soldiers who kept racing round the deck to keep fit.

The convoy was commanded by Admiral Sir Philip Vian. He had made his name as commander of the destroyer HMS *Cossack*, which had boarded a German supply ship, the *Altmark*, which had supplied the Admiral Graf Spee, and was sheltering in a Norwegian fjord before taking British sailors captured by the Admiral Graf Spee back to Germany. The *Cossack* had run up alongside the German ship, and sailors armed with revolvers and knives had boarded her and released the captive British sailors.

I must pay tribute to my immediate superior officer on HMS *Hilary*, Wing Commander Dicky Abrahams, a former fighter pilot. Dicky had a razor-sharp mind and a wonderful sense of humour. He was extraordinarily kind and helpful to me as his second-in-command. I much admired the way he was able to hold his own against superior officers in our meetings in the operation room in the build-up to D Day; he was up against the Admiral's Chief of Staff, who was a Commodore, and the Army Chief of Staff, a Brigadier.

The Hilary had no air conditioning, so as we approached the

Mediterranean the cabins became very hot. Designed for single use, each now had to accommodate four officers, so only one man at a time could wash or shave. As we reached Gibraltar, I found it so hot that I decided to sleep on deck. I spent many comfortable nights under the stars. It occurred to me that if we were torpedoed during the night, all I had to do was put on my life-jacket and slip into the water.

The convoy was protected by an escort of three corvettes and two frigates which sailed alongside us, sometimes on our port side, sometimes on the starboard. Occasionally we heard a depth charge going off, which meant that our defenders had detected an enemy submarine and were trying either to destroy it or to keep it down deep, where it could do no harm.

On entering the Mediterranean our escorting vessels had to refuel at Gibraltar, so for the first couple of days along the North African coast we had to rely on protection from aircraft, which would shadow us from first light until dark. The weather continued very fine and the smooth sea revealed many oil slicks left by all the ships which had been damaged or sunk over the previous three years.

One night, as we were sailing down the coast of Tunisia, I went to bed with the land on my right and woke at first light to find it on my left. It appeared that in the early dawn the convoy had turned round and was now steering the opposite course. One of the naval officers told me this was because the convoy was ahead of schedule and had to lose some time. It may also have been intended to mislead any enemy aircraft which may have detected us – perhaps it would make them think we were steering towards Sardinia or Corsica to the north.

Later that morning we about-turned once more and resumed our voyage down the coast of Tunisia. By midday we had turned north east and were soon in sight of Malta. A very strong westerly now blew up behind us, and by mid-afternoon it had reached gale force. As we steered north past Malta, the wind was so strong that I found it hard to walk on the sloping deck. The sea became rougher and rougher, and we watched the assault craft coming out from Malta disappear in the troughs of huge waves. The soldiers in those little craft would have been pretty seasick by the time they reached the invasion coast of Sicily.

By mid-afternoon it had still not been decided whether the invasion would take place the following morning, because of the force of the wind. We were told a decision would be made by 6 pm, by headquarters staff in Gibraltar or Algiers. They would know before we did when the wind started to drop, as it was coming from the west.

We were told that if the wind abated the landing would take place as planned, at dawn the next morning. Otherwise the convoy would turn round and steam away from Sicily for 12 hours before returning to its original course, delaying the landing by 24 hours.

At six o'clock that evening we were told that the wind was indeed dropping, so we were to follow the original plan. I stayed up all that night, because I wanted to follow our approach to the area where the convoy would anchor and see where the boats would be lowered into the sea to allow the assault troops to land.

One of the Naval officers suggested that I should stand forward so that I could look over the prow and watch for the red light of our marker submarine. The sub had been submerged there for the past three or four days. When it surfaced and showed the red light, this would be the signal for us to move up to within a few hundred yards of it and anchor.

Sure enough, at about 3 am we spotted the red light ahead of us, and heard a rattle of anchor chains as our ship anchored safely. We were about six miles offshore.

The first boats to be hoisted over the side of the ship were two air-sea rescue launches which were stowed above the hatches. But there was still a very heavy swell running, and the first launch smashed into the side of our ship. When they lowered it into the water it was clear that it had been holed. The water poured in, and the launch sank straight to the bottom.

We had better luck with the next one, which was safely floated and sailed away by the RAF crew who would be manning it. Their main task would be to pick up any pilots, RAF or enemy, who had parachuted into the sea around the invasion coast. They would then be able to reach their base in the port of Syracuse.

The convoy was now anchored up over a wide area. Canadian soldiers were clambering down nets hung over the sides of the ships and piling into the assault craft. Long before it was light, they were on their way to their landing places. Fortunately the sea was gradually becoming smoother.

After about an hour, we received reports that the landings had been successful and had met little or no opposition. I had to wait for the return of some of the assault craft, because I was ordered to go ashore and make my way to the airfield at Pachino, a dusty little town in the south-eastern corner of Sicily.

Eventually the first of the assault craft returned and we set off for the shore. It was now getting light. As we sailed inland I saw several big splashes which indicated that our convoy was being shelled, either by long-range artillery or high-level enemy aircraft which we could neither hear nor see. But the shelling was spasmodic, and I felt there was little risk of us being hit.

A few yards off the beach, our craft struck an underwater sandbank. Down went the ramp at the front of the assault craft and the bosun in charge escorted us down into the water, which was three or four feet deep. We plunged through the shallows and up on to the beach. Naturally we got soaking wet, but it didn't matter because the sun was coming up and it soon became very hot.

For my walk towards Pachino, which was about four miles away, I had been warned to keep to vehicle or tank tracks so that I wouldn't step on a mine. It took me about an hour to get there. I had a good look round. As far as I could see, it was clear of booby traps. It would be an ideal landing place for the first fighters which would be giving cover to the Canadian and Allied troops now landing in their thousands at Cape Passero, a small headland on the south-east tip of Sicily.

I returned from the airfield, but I had to wait some time to get aboard a landing craft which would take me back to the ship. I reported that as far as I could see, the airfield was fit to take fighter aircraft immediately. It was likely of course that the reconnaissance squadrons flying from Malta would have already surveyed the airfield and reported back to RAF headquarters.

That afternoon we saw clouds of dust coming from the airfield, revealing that some Kittyhawk fighters belonging to the RAF or South African Air Force were already using it. By the time 20 or 30 fighters had taken off there was an enormous cloud of dust stretching out over the sea to the east.

Wing Commander Abrahams had been ordered to go ashore to act as liaison officer with the headquarters of the 1st Canadian Infantry Division, which was commanded by Major General Simmonds, at that time the youngest Major General in the British forces. Within a few weeks it was clear that General Montgomery had been well satisfied with Simmonds' work and within a few months he was promoted to Lieutenant General. He returned to England to command a Canadian corps taking part in the invasion of Europe.

During the 14 days our convoy remained in position off the Sicilian coast, there was very little for us to do. Some afternoons I was invited to help crew the ship's whaler (lifeboat) in races with the whalers of the other ships, which made it all feel rather like a holiday. In the afternoons we were allowed to swim. Great care was taken to ensure that non-swimmers were not allowed to bathe and that the whaler was always in attendance, ready to haul anyone who was in difficulties out of the water.

We were free to go ashore and walk to the airfield, using a direct course now that we knew it was clear of mines. On my third or fourth visit I watched the troops of the Highland Division which had landed north east of Cape Passero advancing along the main road towards the front, where they would either take up positions alongside the Canadians or take over from the Canadians to allow them to move to the left and advance into the island.

On my second visit to the airfield I found a road leading to the interior. The vehicles which had landed with the Scottish division were belting along it at anything up to 60 mph to compete for the lead. They were Bedford 15 cwt vans, each with anything up to 20 or 30 men clinging on to the outside. It made your hair stand on end to see these Scottish soldiers in such a hurry to get to the enemy. There must have been a senior officer somewhere telling them to get a move on.

One midday I visited the airfield to talk to the Kittyhawk pilots, and then walked on into Pachino. To gain a little respite from the heat I went into the large Catholic church in the main square, finding it delightfully cool. As I walked across the square on my way back, I noticed a narrow street to my left where a line of soldiers stood outside what appeared to be a barber's shop, with a beaded curtain over the entrance. I asked what they were queueing for and was told it wasn't a barber's shop but a house of ill repute. I was told - what do you expect when these men have been two years in the desert?

The area was a hot, arid part of Sicily, where the local people grew tomatoes and poor-quality grapes for the local winery. There were olive trees everywhere. When I went ashore the second time, captured Italian soldiers were working willingly with the British and Canadian soldiers and sailors to unload stores on to the beaches. The Italian men usually wore breeches, but when they saw the British and Canadian men in shorts they cut off the legs of their breeches so that they too could work in comfort in the heat.

When we left Sicily that July our convoy dispersed. HMS Hilary sailed to Algiers to lead further operations against the Italian mainland, including the attack on Anzio which would follow within a few months. At Algiers I was able to obtain authority for a flight back to the UK. I managed to get aboard an American C47 – the aircraft we call a Dakota – headed for Casablanca in Morocco. From Casablanca I hitched a flight to Marrakech, about 150 miles south. After that I had to wait about a week before I could get aboard an American C54, a four-engined Skymaster, which would fly me all the way from Marrakech to Prestwick in Scotland.

We took off from Marrakech just before dark, taking a detour towards the Azores to avoid the German long-range fighters based in western France. I slept quite comfortably on the floor of the aircraft, and was awoken in time for our landing at an airfield near Glasgow.

From Prestwick I was able to get a flight to Hendon. After reporting to the Air Ministry in the late afternoon I caught the 7.10 from Paddington and arrived in Bicester soon after 8 pm.

I had telephoned home so that I could be met at the station in Bicester, and was very soon home with Daphne. I had arrived back in time to take part in the harvest, which was now in full swing in glorious sunny weather. It was July 30 1943.

Before sailing from Gourock, I had despatched a box of kippers to my parents. My father had guessed that this meant I was waiting to board a ship, but neither my parents nor my wife had any idea that I had been taking part in the invasion of Sicily, a key operation in the Allied reclamation of Europe.

London under attack
1943-1944

I thought I would get at least a week's leave after my service overseas, but three days later I received a telegram ordering me to report to Group Headquarters at Redhill. From there I was flown to an airfield at Woodchurch, near Ashford in Kent, where I was to take over No.231 Fighter Reconnaissance Squadron, part of No 39 Canadian Reconnaissance Wing.

The Squadron had been based in Ireland since its formation early in the war, and it had been the last to be equipped with Mustangs. The pilots were very keen, but they needed further training. The AOC told me he would give us extra time to bring the pilots up to a reasonable standard and arranged air firing practice at RAF Shoreham on the south coast. The Wing consisted of three Canadian squadrons and ourselves.

The airfield had been carved out of the Kent countryside. Its two runways had been created by levelling an area of pasture and covering it with steel netting to create what was known as Sommerfeld tracking. This would prevent the wheels from sinking into the ground if it became waterlogged after rain. However, if an aircraft was making a forced landing with the undercarriage up it would rip up yards of expensive tracking, so any aircraft coming back with a damaged undercarriage was ordered to touch down away from the tracking.

We were all accommodated in tents. There was a large one for the officers' mess, a larger one again for the airmen and of course separate tents for the non-commissioned officers. The routine was rather different with these Canadians. Breakfast and lunch were at the usual time but there was no tea at four or five o'clock. Instead they would organise a high tea at about 6-6.30. This allowed flying to continue until around six without interruption.

Our operational role was very similar to the one we had undertaken with 35 Wing - shipping reconnaissance along the coast, photography of German coastal defences and occasional sorties by pairs of aircraft into France or Belgium, where we were allowed to shoot up anything we thought might be German. My first job was to take vertical photographs of enemy airfields. There was no reaction from the Germans, and no anti-aircraft fire.

We also had to photograph the Normandy beaches in preparation for the D-Day landings, although the beaches were not singled out as such, for obvious reasons. We flew parallel to the coast at sea level, about 100 yards to a mile out to sea, to simulate a ship's eye view of the coast. This low-level flying also helped to keep us under the Germans' radar.

In mid-October we were told we would be vacating Woodchurch to move to winter quarters at Redhill in Surrey. By the end of October all the aircraft were accommodated at Redhill, and No.231 Squadron moved into a large, comfortable house on the edge of the airfield. We enjoyed a very pleasant existence, with the town of Redhill not far away and an easy rail journey into London. Many of the Canadians would go into London at six in the evening and return in the early hours of the morning.

With the reorganisation of the Tactical Air Force and the formation of 83 and 84 Groups, it was apparent that three squadrons in each reconnaissance wing would be enough – two Mustang squadrons for low-level reconnaissance and photographic work and one Spitfire squadron, equipped with the Mark XI. These Spitfires were unarmed but carried extra petrol tanks to enable them to range far into Germany at up to 30,000 feet to take photographs. At that height you were considered fairly safe from German aircraft.

No.231 Squadron was therefore no longer needed. The team was disbanded and the pilots sent to other Mustang squadrons. They had been a good lot of chaps, a very happy bunch, and I was sorry to see them split up.

Chapter 9

I was now told that I would join a Department of the Air Ministry which was concerned with the training of tactical reconnaissance pilots. I had to report to Adastral House in Kingsway, where I was told I would be working for the next seven or eight months.

I took up my appointment in the Air Ministry about three weeks before Christmas 1943. My mother's sister, Aunt Dora, and her husband lived in a large detached house at Wallington, near Croydon in Surrey, and invited me to stay with them there.

Aunt Dora's two sons had both been called up and were now serving overseas. Brian had trained as an armourer and was serving with a fighter squadron in the Middle East, while Chris, the younger, was an aerial observer. He trained in aircraft recognition and was sent out to India, where for 12 months he lived in a remote village in Northern Burma, close to the Thai border. There, he and his team of five or six young airmen had to report on any aircraft they saw in the sky and check on the movements and whereabouts of any Japanese soldiers reported by the natives.

It was a very boring job for Chris and his men, as they had little to do all day except improve their "bashas" or huts, which were built from thatch or palm leaves, and scrounge around for food to augment the rations which were dropped to them by air. To communicate with their base at Imphal in northern India they used wireless telegraphy, using morse code. Their equipment was powered with a battery which was charged with a little generator running on petrol. They fixed up a supply of running water by making bamboo pipes to take water from a stream above their little camp.

The nearby village was very primitive. The natives owned only a few chickens and as far as Chris could remember, no other livestock. The only tool for tilling the land was a kind of hoe with a blade about six inches wide, which they would dig into the ground to pull out chunks of earth. These they would break into smaller pieces until eventually they would have a tilth fine enough for planting.

Chapter 9

It was a much more comfortable life for me in London. From Wallington it was an easy journey to the Ministry, with trains running until midnight. I helped to make sure the training was adequate and that there would be enough new pilots to join the squadrons after the invasion of France, when casualties were expected to be high.

It was interesting work. As a Squadron Leader I was allowed to read some of the top secret intelligence reports, so I always had a clear idea of how the war was progressing, especially the air war over Europe.

By early 1944 night bomber raids by the Germans had fallen off. However, one May morning at about five o'clock, I was woken by a terrific crash. I learned later from the intelligence reports that it had been the first of the V1 flying bombs or 'doodlebugs', and it had fallen near Croydon. Poor old Croydon became the most heavily-bombed area in London - although most of the bombs were aimed at the centre of London, many fell short, and Croydon very often got in the way. In all it was hit by around 140 doodlebugs.

From then on we had many sleepless nights. Eventually we moved into an air raid shelter which my aunt and uncle had built in the garden.

One hot and sunny Friday in July 1944, I had a visit at Adastral House from Squadron Leader Lardner-Burke from Fighter Command HQ at Stanmore. I think he was the brother of Desmond Lardner-Burke, who became Legal Advisor to the Rhodesian Prime Minister, Ian Smith.

After our meeting I took Lardner-Burke to lunch in the Surrey, a well-known pub in Surrey Street, Aldwych, on the southern side of the Strand. With lunch over we headed back to the office and began to cross the street opposite W H Smith's (the branch is still there). I noticed my Air Commodore walking along the opposite pavement, and I remember thinking that if we kept our position in front of him we should get to the office first. I also remember looking at my watch and seeing that it was five minutes to two.

As we crossed the street, out of the corner of my eye, I saw silhouetted against the sky the dark outline of a doodlebug. It was perhaps 400 feet up, and diving down straight towards us.

You knew you were in trouble with a V1 when you heard its engine cut out, because there would be a few second's terrible silence, then the blast. However nobody would have heard this one, because of the noise of the traffic. Its engine must have stopped somewhere over Waterloo Station, and it was now heading down straight towards Bush House, the BBC headquarters opposite Adastral House.

I realised that I only had a split second to act. I threw myself down on to the road, and the bomb hit. There was a huge, deafening bang.

I looked up to see dust everywhere. For a moment it was so thick that I couldn't see what was going on around me. I wondered if the buildings were about to collapse. I soon realised they were still standing, but as I looked up I could see a bus bearing down on me, so I got to my feet in a hurry.

As I stood up, a raincoat fluttered down in front of me, and I bent down to pick it up. I stepped forward through the dust and there in front of me was a man lying dead. The blast had stripped him of everything except his underpants. I don't know whether he had been carrying the coat, or wearing it. I looked inside the man's briefcase, which had blown open, and saw that he was an engineer from Metropolitan Vickers in Birmingham, obviously on a visit to London.

All around me in the dust were the forms of dead, dying or injured people, and I began to pick my way among them. None of them seemed to be moving, and I don't remember seeing any blood. It was as if they had all been instantly rendered either dead or insensible by the blast.

I could see exactly where the bomb had struck, just outside the little Post Office. In fact it had fallen on top of a number 11 bus which was parked outside the Post Office, so it had exploded about 15 feet above the road.

Next to Bush House I came to a WRAF officer lying in the road. She was quite dead.   Her skirt must have blown off, poor girl, because I remember noticing that she was wearing Aertex knickers.

Inside the Post Office was a young woman who had been chasing us the night before because we were late on fire-watching duty – she had reported us for staying too long down at the pub and had threatened to file a complaint. I wouldn't have to worry about that now, because she too was dead.

I found my Air Commodore lying badly hurt on the pavement. A taxi had been blown into his path and he had been struck by shards of glass from the windows. The blast also perforated both his eardrums.

Lardner-Burke, however, was completely unscathed.   He had just carried on walking across to the pavement as if nothing had happened. He didn't even suffer any damage to his hearing - I have no idea why. I think my own hearing, already affected in 1940 when we were bombed at Aspelaere, was damaged further.

The rescue services were marvellous - by the time I got to Bush House there were dozens of white-coated doctors, nurses and first-aid people scurrying around tending to the injured. Most of the casualties were out in the street, because the buildings had protected most of those inside, except for the poor girls sunning themselves on the Air Ministry roof in their lunch hour. It was quite a success for the Luftwaffe, and one of the most destructive of all the flying bombs that fell on London. I'm proud to say that it was through photo-reconnaissance sorties that the launch sites for those bombs were discovered and destroyed.

On Fridays we were allowed to finish a little early, so that day I left at five and caught the 6.10 back to Bicester, where I was able to spend a quiet weekend helping with the harvest.

I had told the chaps in the office that I thought well over a hundred people must have died in the blast, but it wasn't quite that bad – when I returned to work on the Monday I was told that the death toll was in fact 82. Nevertheless, Hitler had struck us a terrible and tragic blow.

Chapter 10

Service at the front
1944-45

All leave had been cancelled early in 1944 in preparation for the invasion of France, as it was such a critical time and there was so much to do. In early September we were finally granted our first leave for over eight months. However I had been on leave only a few days when I received a telegram from the Air Ministry telling me they were posting me as Wing Commander (Operations) of 35 Wing, which was now operating in France under the support of the Canadian Army.

After clearing my desk at the Air Ministry, I went off to report to 84 Group Support Unit on an airfield near Andover, where pilots were waiting to reinforce squadrons in France. After a couple of days I was ordered to take a Mustang to 35 Wing's airfield, which was now at St Omer Fort Rouge in Northern France. I was rejoining No.268 Squadron, which along with No.4 Squadron and No.2 Squadron had only a few days previously left the bridgehead in Normandy where they had landed soon after the invasion on June 6.

I received a warm welcome from my old friends in No.268 Squadron and No.4 Squadron. The airfield was a few miles north of Clairmarais, where I had spent my last night in France in 1940. It was quite a coincidence that I was returning to almost exactly the place I had been forced to retreat from four years earlier.

The enemy had been in headlong retreat through France and Belgium for at least a fortnight, but they were now beginning to reform along the Belgian/Dutch frontier. Our job was to reconnoitre the area for retreating German army units and others which might be coming up to the line to reinforce them and help them to make a stand.

Chapter 10

The operation to secure the bridges over the river at Arnhem had begun, and one of my early jobs was to fly a Spitfire XI - one of those which were armed with cameras instead of guns – up to about 20,000 ft to photograph the area. The mission went off without incident, although I felt very exposed in my new role as an unarmed Spitfire pilot 20,000 feet up in a cloudless sky.

We continued with all the usual reconnaissance work, including artillery reconnaissance, which involved directing the guns on to targets which we had located. We were now using a different system. Everything was controlled by the pilot, who would use his radio telephone to give firing instructions and then observe the fall of shot until the shells found the target. The idea had been thought up by John Fuller in No.4 Squadron, and it worked very well. It was later taken up by Army artillery officers, who improved the control system.

After about ten days at St Omer we moved to an airfield near Ghent in Belgium, where the pilots were accommodated in a large house with a big dining room. Most of the airmen were still sleeping in tents, as the weather was still fine, although the nights were getting colder.

After staying in Ghent for about three weeks, we moved to the airfield of Antwerp-Deurne, east of Antwerp, where we stayed until November 1944. The Germans were now directing their V1 flying bombs and V2 rockets at Antwerp docks. Many of the V2s fell close to our airfield and one struck it, making a crater 30 yards across.

At Antwerp-Deurne we used a large stone-built barn with a steep sloping roof as our officers' mess. It served us well, but it was a rather rickety structure and I was afraid that a bomb falling close to the barn might bring it tumbling down.

It was while we were at Antwerp-Deurne that Lord Trenchard, who had been the Chief of the Air Staff for many years and was regarded as the father of the RAF, came to visit us. He was a wonderful old gentleman with an excellent sense of humour, but he was very deaf. Before lunch one day he was enjoying a sherry with Group Captain Anderson, who was in command of 35 Wing, while I was standing a few feet away. Suddenly we heard the sound of an approaching flying bomb. The noise of its engine got louder and louder, and then, just as the sound was above us, we heard the engine cut out.

Group Captain Anderson and I listened intently. We knew the bomb was likely to glide on for a mile or two before landing. As I moved towards the doorway, Anderson threw himself flat on the floor. Lord Trenchard, however, had heard nothing. He was mystified – he could not understand why the Group Captain who had been chatting to him was suddenly lying flat on the ground.

The bomb burst some distance away, and Anderson got back to his feet. We explained to Lord Trenchard what had happened.

At lunchtime I was called away twice to answer the telephone. On my second return, Lord Trenchard said to me: "You don't have to get the waiter to call you to the phone to show how important you are. I know all these manoeuvres. During the First World War I once got an engineer officer to bring me part of an engine while we were lunching with some of our senior officers, so I know what you fellows get up to impress a senior officer."

We stayed at Antwerp until just before Christmas, when we moved up to Gilze-Rijen. This was a very large airfield which had been built with Dutch labour to the orders of the German forces soon after they occupied Holland in 1940; it was used as a base for the Germans while they were bombing England. The accommodation, which was about a mile from the airfield itself, was excellent. We had good baths and a fully-working water system.

The airfield had been heavily and accurately bombed by the American day bombers, so the whole area was covered with bomb craters. The Army engineers quickly filled them in and repaired the runways, which were made of red Dutch bricks laid on a sand base so that surface water would percolate through into the ground. It was a good way to build a runway quickly and it was easily repaired, although too many repairs would leave it rather uneven.

Early in December my wing headquarters was instructed to pick up a Mustang IV, belonging to an RAF Polish squadron which had force landed at Charleroi, an American base. It had been repaired by the Americans and was ready to be returned to its squadron at Odiham.

I picked up the aircraft at Charleroi and took off from a mud-saturated, steel-planked runway on the morning of December 7, after waiting all night for the rain to stop. In fact, two mud-splattered Americans cleaned the windshield for me at the last minute, so I could see for take-off. But instead of flying direct to Odiham I diverted to RAF Bicester, flying in over the cottage hospital, where Daphne had just given birth to our second daughter, Marijoy. I delivered the Mustang to Odiham later that day and was back at the battle front by evening.

We spent a very pleasant Christmas at Gilze-Rijen; our only concern was the build-up of German forces just a few miles away on the other side of the Rhine. If they had wanted to, the Germans could have mounted an armed raid across the river and taken our airfield at any moment. After the war we learned that the original German plan was indeed to have included an attack on us. In the event they concentrated all their forces on an attack on the American forces in the Ardennes.

Most of the time it was a pleasant existence. We enjoyed comfortable quarters and excellent food. We even found a supply of oysters, thanks to a fishery at Bergen-Op-Zoom. They were inspected by our medical officers, who assured us they were safe to eat.

It wasn't until New Year's Day 1945 that we came under attack, from about 20 German fighter aircraft. This was part of a major Luftwaffe assault in which some 500 fighters attacked all the RAF and US stations within easy distance of the battle area. Two of our pilots who were on reconnaissance behind enemy lines that morning came across a large formation of German fighters flying west towards the Dutch coast, where they turned left towards Belgium before turning inland to attack airfields at Ghent, Northern France and near Brussels. They noticed that one pilot was lagging behind, and easily shot him down - the first German fighter to fall to our pilots.

The attack started at about eight in the morning. I was in the timber-built operations building when I heard the rattle of machine guns and dashed outside to see some 20-30 German fighters swooping down to attack our planes. The airfield housed three wings, each of about three squadrons, so there were well over a hundred aircraft on the airfield. However, at the end of the raid we found that only three had been damaged. Those young German pilots were poorly trained and weren't much good. They did hit one of our Mustangs as it landed; three or four bullets had raked the aircraft from the tail to just behind the cockpit, but fortunately he was unscathed.

Group Captain Anderson had been away celebrating New Year's Eve in Ghent, so that morning I was in charge of the wing. The AOC telephoned me in the ops room, very agitated as he had learned that a large number of aircraft had been destroyed on the airfield occupied by our group at Eindhoven. I was able to reassure him that our attack appeared to be over, that we had suffered no losses and that we had even shot down one German fighter, while another had taken a direct hit from one of our Bofors guns. I watched that aircraft straighten up and glide down the far side of the airfield. The pilot was captured and brought back to the station that morning.

The day was not over, however. That afternoon I saw an old friend of mine killed in a landing accident as he was returning in his Spitfire. He hit one of the badly-repaired bomb craters on the runway and bounced back into the air. In trying to correct his landing, he gave the engine too much throttle and the aircraft turned upside down and slid along the runway; he was killed instantly.

The unfortunate pilot was Flight Lieutenant Garland, the elder brother of Donald Garland, who had been a pilot officer at Bicester just before the war; I had got to know Donald well, because he drank most evenings in the King's Arms. He had been awarded a posthumous Victoria Cross, the first RAF VC of the war, after leading an attack against the Maastricht Bridges in Belgium on May 12 1940. They were flying in a Fairey Battle, a slow, rather cumbersome light bomber, and they were shot down. Donald was buried in the cemetery at Louvain.

Flight Lt Garland was a captain in the Green Howards, a regiment which was stationed near York, and had been attached to my flight in 1940 for flight experience as he had already applied to transfer from the Army to the Royal Air Force. He had been anxious to avenge the death of his brother.

There were two other Garland brothers, and all four were killed serving with the RAF during the war. For many years I had a photograph taken in 1940 of Flight Lieutenant Garland wheeling his mother in her wheelchair through Buckingham Palace to receive his dead brother's Victoria Cross from His Majesty the King. What an awful tragedy to lose all four of your sons like that. I'm sure she would simply say how proud she was that they had died for their country.

If the operation at Arnhem to secure a bridge across the Rhine to allow British and Canadian forces to enter Germany had been successful, the war might have ended much earlier. Unfortunately it failed, so the next operation for the Army was to work with the American forces to the south of us to clear the area west of the Rhine. The English and American forces and the Polish Armoured division maintained a close watch on the enemy while preparations were made to clear the Reichwald Forest to the east of the Dutch border.

Chapter 10

The frosty weather continued, and at first the hard ground made the work easy. However, soon after the British and Canadian attack had started, a thaw set in, and very soon the terrain became impossible for wheeled vehicles and difficult even for tanks. The battle of the Reichwald was to prove very hard going. The Germans were well dug-in in easily-defended country which was wooded and hilly. It included a wall of fortifications called the West Wall, which they had built to defend Germany against any invasion from the west.

It was also difficult and dangerous reconnaissance work for our pilots, who were often flying at very low levels in low cloud and drizzle. They put in sterling work in bringing back vital information despite the conditions.

With the Battle of the Reichwald over, the build-up began to the crossing of the Rhine. We had moved up from Gilze-Rijen to a hastily-prepared airfield at a small Dutch village called Mill. It had been constructed quickly by British engineers using huge vehicles known as graders, with which they could level off large areas of sandy ground, the easiest to work with. They could produce an airfield with a single runway in two or three days. The sand was covered with interlocking plates of steel. The moment an aircraft landed on these there came a deafening clanking noise, which stopped again the moment it took off. It was quite frightening until you got used to it.

While we were at Mill, the British and Canadian armies were closing up on the River Rhine. Group Captain Anderson said he wanted to cross the river as soon as the first pontoon bridge was completed, at Wesel, to see what damage had been done to the town, an important riverside port. The opportunity to cross depended on luck, as often the traffic was only allowed as far as the river. Once you had crossed you might have to wait a couple of days before you could get back again, because of the reinforcements pouring across the river in pursuit of the Germans.

Chapter 10

We set off in two Jeeps. I boarded one with one of the pilots, while Anderson got into the other with a WAAF officer he had picked up from Ghent airfield the previous day in a two-seater Mustang he had borrowed from the Americans. Her name was Brenda.

As we crossed we were warned by a Redcap (a Military Police officer) that we should not delay our return, as that evening an armoured division would begin crossing the river. Once it had started to cross, no traffic would be allowed in the opposite direction.

We drove through Wesel and headed east out of the town on a road which had been badly damaged by bombs and shellfire. It was the southern boundary of the area into which our paratroopers and glider-borne troops had been dropped. As we continued into Germany we began to spot broken gliders. Some of them had obviously ploughed into one another and crashed to the ground as they tried to land. These were British gliders taking part in an operation to land airborne forces, each with 15-20 men on board. The paratroopers would have landed first to guide the gliders down.

Many dead Germans were still lying in the ditches along the road and surprisingly, we also saw bodies out in open fields. I wondered how these men could have allowed themselves to be shot out in the open when they could have been operating from defensive positions in ditches or the edges of woods.

We saw no British dead. Presumably they had all been collected up already and removed to hospital or for burial.

After driving for half an hour we came to a main road. On our left was a German farmstead, and we could see the farmer standing at the iron gates. We stopped to see if he spoke any English, but all he could say was "Deutschland kaput, Hitler kaput". As far as he was concerned, the war was over.

While we stood at the junction, three Army lorries turned up, discharging some 200 soldiers, a company of the Somerset Light Infantry. We saw a sergeant major posting two Bren gunners to cover the roads in all directions - an example of the care the Army was taking with "all round defence" in enemy territory. We had been talking to them for about ten minutes when one of the soldiers exclaimed "Look, it's a bloody woman!". He had noticed Brenda's curls under her WAAF cap.

We were advised by a captain who appeared to be in command of the troops not to go any further, as he didn't know how far away the enemy was. We could hear no firing. In fact it was hard to believe as we stood there in the early spring sunshine that a major war was being fought only a few miles to the east.

The captain explained that they were moving into position ready to make an attack early the next morning. He thought they faced a long march before they would come into contact with the enemy.

We got back to Wesel in good time to cross the pontoon bridge. Some Marine commandos who had been responsible for taking the town - they had been the first men to cross the river and engage the enemy at bayonet point - told us that they had very few casualties. The operation had gone very well and had proved less difficult than they had expected.

I gave half a dozen of them a lift in my Jeep to get them nearer to their destination near Eindhoven. One of them, a cockney lad, pulled up his arm and showed me three or four wrist-watches which he said he had taken from the inhabitants. "It ain't in the book sir, but these are the spoils of war" he said. The commandos were very grateful for their lift. We took them to within a few miles of their destination and dropped them off to complete their journey on foot.

The battle for the Rhine Bridges started on March 21 1945 and was over within two or three days. After that we were ordered to move to a large German airfield on the border, called Twente-Enschede. This was another airfield built with Dutch labour to provide a base for the German heavy bombers. The Dutch people had had no choice but to comply. If they refused, the Germans would withhold their ration books, or ensure their families suffered in one form or another. As a last resort they could be sent off to a concentration camp.

While we were at Twente-Enschede one of my pilots, Flight Lieutenant Mayne, said his brother would be coming to dinner, having just returned from a sortie by Jeep into German occupied territory. The brother turned out to be Lieutenant Colonel Blair "Paddy" Mayne, a founder member of the SAS, who by this time had been awarded four DSOs. Mayne pioneered the use of military Jeeps to conduct surprise hit-and-run raids, and there have been several campaigns over the years to have his achievements properly recognised with the retrospective award of the VC.

The armistice was signed while we were still at Twente-Enschede, and it was from that airfield that I undertook my last operational sortie of the war. I was due to go on leave when Group Captain Anderson, who was just about to take off, suddenly found he didn't have a No. 2 to be the second pilot. There was nobody in the flight office or the ops room, so I told him: "Right, I'll come, it'll only be an hour and a half".

Anderson had orders to reconnoitre the area around Bremen and then go on to the German island of Borkum and report on any shipping movements along the coast. We could see that a battle was still raging around Bremen. A minute or two after we passed Borkum, Anderson asked if I had got any photographs of it. I explained that I hadn't, as I had only a port-facing camera.

"OK" he said. "If we go back you'll have Borkum on your left." I made a quick turn and flew back to Borkum, passing it at about 2000 feet very fast. I got some good pictures of the harbour and some flashes of anti-aircraft fire, but nothing very detailed.

We flew along the sea between the north German coast and the Dutch islands, and the CO fired a few shots at what looked like Dutch fishing boats. I thought it was unnecessary at this stage in the war to be attacking such small boats, but he would never miss an opportunity to have a crack at anything he thought might be German.

When we reached the Zuiderzee I had to turn back to photograph a very large breach in the dykes just inside the great barrier that separated the Zuiderzee from the North Sea - the Germans had blown the dykes and flooded the whole of the area, famous for growing the most beautiful flowers in Northern Europe. The water was pouring through a hole which must have been 100 to 200 yards wide. I got good pictures of this, though unfortunately I didn't keep copies of them.

We landed back at Twente-Enschede safely and I was able to go on leave. On May 8, within two or three days of my reaching home, the Armistice was signed. The war was over.

Chapter 11

Liberation and homecoming
1945-46

As soon as I rejoined my wing at Twente-Enschede, we were ordered to an airfield near Celle in Germany. Celle was about 12 miles from the concentration camp at Belsen, which had been liberated by the British Army on April 16. They found some 10,000 unburied dead and 20,000 starving inmates.

We were able to get first-hand knowledge of what had gone on at Celle, and we were allowed to visit the camp once the typhus which had been rampant there had been brought under control. Seeing the horror of the camp for the first time turned my stomach, but it justified every single day that I had spent fighting in the war.

Many of the SS guards and Gestapo at Belsen were taken into custody and imprisoned in the civilian prison at Celle, where they were guarded by the original German warders, now serving loyally under Canadian officers. When we visited the prison, we were allowed to watch and photograph the Belsen warders as they exercised. The German civilian staff at the prison served the Canadians loyally and seemed to enjoy working with them.

The Army was engaged in burning down the wooden huts in an attempt to sterilise the place, and the smell of the smoke helped to disguise the stench of decaying bodies. All that remained of the huts were the brick fireplaces.

One afternoon when I visited the prison with a couple of our pilots, the senior wardress asked me if I would like to interview any of the prisoners. We knew that one of the women was the notorious Irma Grese, who had been dubbed the 'Blonde Beast of Belsen', so we asked if we could see her.

The wardress took us to Grese's cell, unlocked the door and shouted to Grese to come to the door. She appeared in a green uniform with a tunic and a split skirt, and I thought she looked a most attractive young lady. She was blonde and pretty and looked no more than about 21 – as indeed she was. It was hard to believe she had patrolled the camp with an Alsatian, whip in hand, setting the dog on to any prisoner who failed to carry out her orders quickly enough.

I asked her how long she had been in the SS, and was told she had joined just over two years ago. Most of that time she must have been at Belsen. She had seen the inmates dying like flies from illness, disease and starvation, but claimed she had been unable to do anything about it. In fact the testimony of the survivors revealed that she had been guilty of the most appalling brutality, torturing inmates, beating women to death and arbitrarily shooting prisoners in cold blood.

Irma Grese was later hanged for her crimes, as was the camp chief, Kommandant Kramer. I attended the trial at the Lüneburg courthouse. She was the youngest woman to be executed under English law in the 20th century.

Food supplies had been cut off some weeks before the camp was liberated. Kommandant Kramer could of course have opened the gates and let those who were fit enough out into the countryside to forage for food. When we interviewed some of the inmates after they were removed from Belsen and given food and clothing, they told us it would have been relatively simple to stay alive out in the countryside.

I took two of our Polish officers and our senior medical officer to interview survivors, as the Polish officers were keen to question any Poles who might have been able to give them news of their families in Poland. Two pretty young Polish girls, aged about 21, invited us back to their small room in the German barracks, where they were pleased to give us an account of their experiences as prisoners of the SS. They had been arrested in Poland and sent to Auschwitz, where Kramer had been the deputy Kommandant. As the advancing Russians approached Auschwitz, it was evacuated by the Germans and the two Polish girls had been put on transports to the west. They ended up at Belsen, where by this time Kramer was in charge.

On arrival they were inspected by Kramer, who tapped them on the shoulder with his cane and said, "I remember you from Auschwitz." No doubt this was because of their good looks.

We asked the girls how they had managed to remain so fit when so many were starving. They said that they had always volunteered to work in the fields, because it gave them the chance to scavenge beet, carrots or cabbages and smuggle them back to the camp to cook over improvised fires. They would cut the rotten parts from rejected potatoes, swedes, turnip or sugar beet and eat the remainder raw or boiled. Of course they had to make sure the guards didn't find out.

The Belsen survivors were taken to the barracks which had housed German officers at Bergen-Belsen, and here they were able to recuperate fairly quickly thanks to better food, accommodation and washing. At first we tried taking them chocolate and cigarettes, but we were told such luxuries could kill them as they had been on starvation rations for so long. They had to be fed little and often. Nevertheless, each time we arrived the children would recognise our car and come running to us, and we could give them tiny amounts of chocolate.

We were amazed to find that many of these children, some as young as six, seemed quite unscathed mentally and appeared to be as happy as any normal children. My mind went back to the day nearly 20 years before when as a child of ten I had watched our farmhouse and all our buildings destroyed by fire. By the time that day was over, all I possessed in the world was what I'd been wearing when I got up in the morning. I had seen my mother in tears, yet I had taken the destruction of our home in my stride. So it was, it seemed, with these children.

Through the grounds of the barracks there ran a pretty little stream, where the women would wash their clothes. It was a hot summer, and some of them thought nothing of bathing naked. They seemed to have lost all sense of modesty as they splashed about in the stream or lay on its banks sunbathing.

One of my proudest moments came about three weeks after the Armistice, when I led my Wing of 36 aircraft, along with another 160 or so fighter-reconnaissance Spitfires and Mustangs, in a victory formation over Germany. It was called "showing the flag", and was intended to demonstrate to the Germans that we still had plenty of aircraft left.

Back at Celle, our own accommodation was excellent. Celle was a very pretty town with some charming houses which were still in fine condition although they dated back to the 15th and 16th centuries. The German domestic staff seemed to be grateful for the opportunity to work for us, partly because it gave them a chance to get hold of some extra food. There was very little available to the Germans in the shops.

We occupying forces felt we were living in the lap of luxury. We enjoyed excellent rations, accompanied by plenty of wine appropriated from the Germans who had stolen them in France. We enjoyed short periods of leave at holiday centres in Bad Harzburg and other German skiing resorts.

The Germans were short of wheat and rye to make bread. This was partly because the occupying forces from Britain, France, Germany, America and particularly Russia had been late releasing German farm workers from the prison camps to gather in their harvest. The British, French and Americans played fair with the Germans, but we were told the Russians were taking all the wheat and barley harvested in eastern Germany back home with them, so the Germans in the Russian-occupied zone were even hungrier than those in the British, French and American zones.

Chapter 11

The Germans in the American zone were probably the best off, as the American soldiers seemed to have better rations. The Americans set up a black market which benefited the Germans in the area. General Montgomery, who was now in supreme command of the British forces, was aware how well the British and Canadian soldiers were living and ordered a reduction in rations, particularly for British officers. No meal in a British officers' mess must exceed three courses - soup, a main dish and a pudding. This, I think, was quickly recognised as a sensible move by the British, and most Germans were impressed by the steps being taken to improve their lot.

All those working in the officers' mess worked loyally for the occupying forces. The German resident engineer who was responsible for maintaining the water supply, electricity supply and sewage for the station was as co-operative as any Englishman would have been if we had been stationed back home.

I went back to Germany at the end of 1945 and in the November I was appointed to command a German research station called Braunschweig-Volkenrode, near Braunschweig (Brunswick). The activity of the research station was led by Göttingen University and it was equipped with the most modern engineering tools - there were planers, grinders and machine tools of every description, bought or commandeered from France, Belgium, Spain, Italy, even Russia.

The Americans who liberated the station sent their engineers and aeronautical experts to look at the place, because it had a wind tunnel big enough to take a German fighter. The wind speed reached 500 mph, which enabled them to observe and measure the airflow over the wing of an aircraft in flight. They also had the first supersonic wind tunnel, 300 feet in diameter, in which they could place wing sections and observe air flow at speeds faster than sound. The Americans were very impressed.

Soon after I arrived at Volkenrode, it was agreed in London that British engineers and scientists should go there to continue the research work which had been done by the German staff before it was liberated by the Americans and handed over to the British. A huge variety of machine tools and other scientific equipment, worth millions of pounds, were to be divided between the four victorious powers.

The British contingent comprised engineers and scientists from the Ministry of Aircraft Production and the Ministry of Supply. They wore blue or khaki uniforms and were granted equivalent ranks while serving in Germany. When lines of research had reached a satisfactory conclusion, the British researchers would continue the work back in England.

Many of the more important German researchers were offered positions at the Royal Aircraft Establishment in Farnborough. At least five professors accepted the invitation and moved there. The British engineers decided that they would rebuild the large wind tunnel, which was known as the Hermann Goering Kanal, at Cranfield, near Bedford, and the powerful Siemens electric motors would be dismantled and incorporated in the British site.

The chief British scientist asked me to collect five Siemens engineers from Gatow airport in Berlin and fly them to Volkenrode to assist with the dismantling of the engines. When I asked Group HQ for permission to arrange my flight to Berlin, the Senior Air Staff Officer (SASO) was aghast at the suggestion, claiming it was strictly against the Potsdam Agreement. I said that it was considered absolutely necessary for future British aeronautical research that the equipment be moved to the UK and the German engineers would be essential to achieving that. I told them that in spite of the risks involved, I was prepared to undertake the flight.

The SASO said, "If anything goes wrong, we will deny that we know anything about you." With that I arranged to fly to Berlin the following day, and I picked up five elderly Germans and their suitcases at Gatow. They appeared to be delighted to be leaving Berlin. It was a beautiful sunny day and I think the Germans enjoyed their 40-minute flight from

Gatow to Volkenrode in an obsolete British aircraft.

There were workshops the size of aircraft hangars and a large grassed airfield. The domestic staff were well housed in accommodation within the camp, which was surrounded by 15 miles of iron fence. The kitchen was equipped with stainless steel boilers in which huge quantities of cabbages, potatoes and other food could be cooked. It was all kept in spotless condition by the German civilian staff, who had happily thrown in their lot with the occupying forces.

Some of the younger members of the domestic staff could not believe the reports now being published in the German press about the death camps. Two young waitresses in our mess would not believe me when I insisted that I had seen and spoken to people who had suffered in the camps. They said, "Ah, British propaganda!" Clearly they were still worshipping Hitler. I asked them whether they had ever seen him, and they told me that they had attended two rallies at the Sportpalast in Berlin, but then one corrected herself and said, "I didn't see him, my eyes were full of tears of admiration."

One dark, freezing night just before Christmas 1945 I was travelling from Volkenrode back to my old Squadron based at Celle airfield. As I approached Celle, I saw that a 15 cwt Army truck had collided with a little four-wheeled farm trolley drawn by an old man and two women. There were no lights on the trolley and they were all in dark clothing. The driver may well have been slightly under the weather because of the Christmas festivities. The truck contained firewood, which appeared to be ash, oak or beech branches four or five inches thick. The ends of the branches were pointed where they had been cut and I found that one of these pointed ends had struck one of the women and had been driven deep into her thigh. She was in great pain, and there was a lot of blood.

Very carefully we lifted the poor woman away from the branch. I told the old man, who was an Alsatian and therefore spoke French, that I would take them all to the hospital in Celle if they would get into the car. This they readily did. I also told the lorry driver to come with me and to take the other two back to where we had found them, once we had seen their friend safely to the hospital.

The old man knew exactly where the civil hospital in Celle was. When we drew up to the door it was clear Christmas festivities were in full swing - the staff were swinging lanterns and walking round one of the wards singing Silent Night, or rather Stille Nacht, very much as they do in England. The old man got hold of a doctor and a nurse, and they quickly took the dear old lady away and took care of her.

A few weeks later I received an official letter from the driver's regiment asking me to fill in an accident report form and to indicate whether he had been under the influence of alcohol. I stated only that I had smelled drink on his breath and told them exactly what I had seen from the short period he was with me. I've often wondered how many German officers would have taken as much care of the local people in the countries they had occupied.

I stayed at Volkenrode for the whole of that winter, which gave me the opportunity to go skiing in the Harz mountains. In the spring of 1946 I was able to join the gliding club at Salzgitter, which was only a 20-minute drive away. It was a most enjoyable summer, but all good things have to come to an end, and in August I was notified that my release from the RAF was now confirmed and that I should return to the UK.

At Volkenrode I had been allocated an old Anson aircraft for communication purposes and I flew this back to Farnborough with my old friend Flying Officer Red Kelly, who had also been notified of his release. Once again I was lucky enough to reach home in time to assist with the harvest, as I had often been able to do during the previous six years.

Back home in England, I reflected on how much I had enjoyed my time serving in Germany and began to think about applying for a regular commission. However, farming was still my life. One day towards the end of 1946 when I was home on leave, I had a visit from Richard Collett from Hawkwell Farm. He told me he had always enjoyed talking with me when I had been home on leave and had given him a hand with the haymaking or the harvest. I in turn said I had been grateful to him for allowing Fred Jeacock to give my father a hand, even letting us cut the standing hay crop and corn with their machinery.

We had been reduced to quite a small acreage after giving up Gowell Farm and Copthall Farm, which amounted to a loss of about 200 acres. Now Mr Collett said he was planning to buy Hawkwell Farm from his landlord, and he would be happy to sell 50 acres of it on to me acting for my father. His son-in-law, Tom Ward, was thinking of joining him and he didn't think the farm would generate enough money for the two of them. He said he would give me the first chance of the land because of my war service.

The conversation reawoke my interest in farming, and I began to reconsider my plan to continue with the RAF.

I should mention at this point how fortunate we had been, compared to some farmers I knew. This was the time when the Government had decided to make sure the land was being used as productively as possible by penalising any farmer who was found guilty of 'poor husbandry'. It was all administered by the County Agricultural Committees and their smaller Area Committees, which were in full swing by 1941. 'Poor husbandry' could mean failing to thatch a rick in good time, or not controlling weeds, though there were very few sprays in those days that could be used safely on farms. If you were found guilty you were thrown out – even if it was your own farm. There was no appeal against an eviction order. The whole family could be turned out with nowhere to go.

The Oxfordshire County Committee had offices on the Marston Road on the outskirts of Oxford, and it employed agricultural advisers, veterinary officers, horticultural advisers and of course plenty of clerks to do all the correspondence. The chairman was Ted Withington, who lived at Fringford Lodge near Bicester. He was a retired racehorse trainer who had trained a horse called Rubio, which had won the Grand National in 1908. He farmed only a very small place of his own and seemed to be unaware of some of the evictions which were taking place in his area

The smaller Area Committees were chaired by local farmers. They were not always men of integrity, and there were cases of good men being forced out of their farms under the pretext of poor husbandry and those same farms then being occupied by close friends or relatives of committee members. Later on this legislation came to be recognised as one of the wickedest miscarriages of justice in agricultural history.

One local example was Archie Busby, whose children were great friends of mine. He had six of the prettiest daughters in Bicester, while the youngest was a son. He lost his farm on some pretext, so he moved a few miles across the county boundary into Buckinghamshire. His record for 'poor husbandry' didn't follow him into Buckinghamshire, which had a different committee of course, and he was able to take on a little farm there and eke out a living for the rest of the war. His farm was nearly all grass, producing beef and mutton for many years and part of it was heavy clay covered with barely three inches of topsoil.

Near us was a dairy farm owned and run by two bachelor brothers, Bert and David Harris. They sold milk by the pint or half pint from a dairy in North Street to people who brought their jugs or cans along. In early 1942 the committee issued them with an order requiring them to plough up 25 acres of grass and plant wheat by 31 October.

The land had been down to grass for 50 years or more and the brothers had no machinery, ploughs or harrows. There was no way they could comply with the order, so as they were both in their sixties they decided to retire. They had two nephews who would have been able to take on the farm, but both had been called up, so the farm had to be sold. When it was sold on again around 1960, it went for housing and fetched £14m. It was a scandalous loss to the Harris family.

Another victim was was an aged farmer called Charlie Haynes. Charlie had taken Simms Farm, a very good farm on the Middleton Estate (formerly owned by the Jersey family), a few years before the war, when farming was unprofitable. He took it on at five shillings an acre, because the landlords were desperate to find tenants who would take the land, farm it and keep it in some sort of order.

Now that war had started and farming was more lucrative, there were other farmers looking enviously at Mr Haynes. He was accused of poor husbandry because he had grown broad beans and peas in his fields and asked local people to come and pick their own and pay by the pound. This was a new practice to the older members of the committee and they didn't like it. The truth is, Charlie Haynes was ahead of his time - he was one of the first people to introduce pick-your-own as a method of growing a crop for human consumption.

Charlie's sense of enterprise didn't impress the committee. It wasn't long before he was presented with an eviction order and dispossessed, spending the last few years of his life in a wooden hut.

It was odd that neither the estate landlord nor his agent ever intervened to support their tenant. Even if they had of course, it's likely that they would have been overruled by the committee, whose members were full of self-importance and in some cases drunk with power.

An old schoolmate of mine, a farmer from Bletchingdon, joined in the game of dispossessing other farmers with great abandon. I recall him telling me how an elderly farmer on the Shelswell estate had had the temerity to stand up to two members of the committee who had inspected his farm. He was called in to give a third opinion, and of course he agreed with his fellow committee members that the standard of husbandry was not good enough and that the man should be forced out. What could that poor farmer do? He had lost his livelihood and his home, flung out on to the road by a group of his fellow farmers.

Ted Withington, as chairman, must have know what was going on, as he would have had to sign the certificate confirming that the farmer was guilty of poor husbandry. Yet I know of no cases where he intervened to suggest that if a farmer had managed to keep his farm going all through the depression years, he could not be so bad at his job.

There were some men of integrity on these committees. I remember talking to a Mr Pickford, who farmed at Upper Heyford and was a member. He told me he had once or twice intervened on behalf of a farmer who was being unfairly dispossessed, but he was always overruled.

Ministry of Agriculture officers stationed in Oxford were given authority to set up depots where machinery was stored ready for hire to farmers who hadn't been able to buy, for example, a binder or a mowing machine. Later in the war they also had tractors for hire. I recall one farmer towards the end of the war trying to hire a binder to complete his harvesting. The man in charge of the depot said their only binder had been taken by the chairman of the local committee, just in case his own binder broke down. That's the kind of thing the committees got up to.

The dreadful unfairness of all these actions was not fully recognised until 1954, when the notorious Crichel Down affair made the national headlines. Crichel Down was a 700-acre estate in Wiltshire owned by the third Baron Alington, a serving RAF officer. In 1938 part of the estate was compulsorily purchased by the Air Ministry, to be used for training purposes. In 1940, the Baron was killed on active service.

Soon after the war ended, the estate was de-requisitioned and handed to the Ministry of Agriculture, which put up the price of the land beyond the amount the original owners could afford and leased it out, despite an earlier promise from Sir Winston Churchill that land would be returned to its owners after the war, when it was no longer required for the purpose for which it had been bought. The owners campaigned successfully for a public inquiry and Crichel Down was finally returned to them; the Minister responsible, Sir Thomas Dugdale, resigned, accepting full responsibility for the affair.

Another aspect of wartime farming in our locality was the black marketeering of agricultural produce. Almost all commodities produced for human consumption were controlled and rationed. If a farmer could find someone to butcher a calf, lamb, sheep or pig on the farm, he could sell joints on the black market to friends whom he could trust to keep their mouths shut. Sheep were the easiest - the only difficulty was disposing of the fleece. If the police arrived, you said you'd had to bury a sheep which had died from disease or difficult lambing, but saved the fleece. It was quite easy to pin a fleece to a board to dry it out and turn it into a nice warm rug.

There was another dodge people used to try to save wheat for their chickens. Because wheat was so valuable for making bread, which was in short supply, every sack of wheat which was thrashed out in the rickyard had to be accounted for. The threshing contractor had to make a return to the County Agricultural Committee of the number of sacks thrashed out every day. However, many farmers wanted to keep back a fair supply of wheat to feed to their chickens, because eggs and poultry could easily be sold on the black market for inflated prices. So they would put two or three loads of wheat at the bottom of a rick and then build the rest up from oats or barley. The threshing contractor could then report that he had thrashed out 80 sacks of barley, not 70 sacks of barley and ten of wheat.

I can recall only one prosecution for black marketeering, of a man who had killed a pig without a licence. He was found guilty, but the fine was not very large.

Fuel rationing brought transport difficulties to the farming community. When the Derby was moved from Epsom to the safer course at Newmarket, many a cattle lorry would arrive there loaded not with livestock but with a group of farmers out for a day's racing. It must have been uncomfortable, but they thought it well worthwhile for a day at the races.

I continued to do my best to make Lords Farm successful. Late in 1946 we bought some lambs at Buckingham Sheep Fair and put them to graze on a mixture of red clover and trefoil which had been undersown with our wheat in early spring. It's an unusual mixture – perhaps my father just happened to have the seeds in the barn - but it grew into a rich-looking aftermath, ideal for fattening lambs.

They were not the best of lambs when we bought them, but they improved rapidly on their new forage and grew well until late December, when we had the first hard frost. A few days later we had deep snow, so we brought them back to a field near Lords Farm and finished them on rolled oats. When we took them to market, only half the lambs were graded as fit for the subsidy available on finished animals, so we brought the rest back to finish them.

In early December, just before we moved the lambs, I had a call from Group Captain Anderson, who was now at a desk in the Air Ministry. He told me he had seen an Air Ministry Order that I had been granted a regular commission. I told him I was now back in farming, and wasn't planning to return to the RAF.

Anderson wasn't put off by that. He explained that he was head of a directorate which was concerned with accident prevention in the RAF, and he had a "most interesting job" to offer me. They had mounted a large exhibition which was visiting all the RAF bases in the UK. They were now adapting this into an airborne exhibition and they needed an officer who was prepared to spend eight months travelling overseas to visit every RAF station between Gibraltar and Australia.

There were no volunteers within the directorate, as many officers were prepared to do a three-month stint but were reluctant to be away for longer. Yet this was a wonderful opportunity to see the world. I would be able to visit, as he put it, "every RAF station that had been involved in fighting the war from 1939 to 1945".

I told him I would study the conditions for my return and let him know. I had a number of things to sort out at home, so I kept him waiting for a few days, but finally I replied that I would accept the offer of a permanent commission and could rejoin at the end of January. It was too interesting an opportunity to turn down.

I had just engaged a local architect to build a bungalow on a plot next to the orchard at Lords Farm, and I needed to instruct the builder. I was keen to move my wife and children to the new house so that they would no longer be an encumbrance to my in-laws. Delighted as Daphne's parents had been to accommodate them, I felt it was a bit unfair on them, and of course my wife would be only too pleased to have a house of her own.

The deep frost continued into 1946. The weather was making life difficult for Mr Collett as well – he had started threshing a couple of wheat ricks, but the conditions made it a slow business and then his spring ploughing was delayed by a sudden thaw in mid March. On March 19, when I was home on leave and ploughing in one of our fields, I got bogged down in a wet patch – most unusual in Cotswold brash, which normally drains quickly. We were late planting that field with spring barley, and Mr Collett was even later. By the time he had managed to finish planting his spring corn it was well into early April.

Barley planted in April was known as 'cuckoo barley', because that was the time when the cuckoo appeared. If you had cuckoo barley and it was a dry summer, you could expect a poor crop. So it was for Mr Collett. One field produced just a single load of sheaves, each barely a foot high.

Later that year he explained to me that the 1947 harvest had been so poor after the dry summer that it hadn't even covered his income tax on the previous year's earnings.

It was while I was on leave from the RAF in 1946 that I finally managed to get an electricity supply connected to the farm. The new Labour Government had introduced subsidies to get electricity to isolated farms, so it was no longer such a costly exercise. I remember that I had to pay about £80 to the electricity board to make the connection and to guarantee them that we would use at least another £80 a year in electricity. I knew we would use far more than that, thanks to the introduction of milking machines and other electrical equipment.

With the arrangements made for the construction of my new home, I returned to the RAF at the end of January 1947 and checked in at RAF Uxbridge before joining Group Captain Anderson in the Deputy Directorate for Accident Prevention's offices in Kingsway.

Andy Anderson arranged for me to have a quick refresher course at RAF Bentwaters in Suffolk, where I got experience on Mosquitos and one trip on a Hornet, an aircraft which had only just been designed and built as the war ended. While there I heard the news that Daphne had given birth to our first son, whom we named John. I left the course the next day to visit him and Daphne back in Bicester, and was pleased to find them both doing well.

World tour
1947-48

The Directorate of Accident Prevention (DAP) had been formed towards the end of the war because the expansion of the RAF was being held back by an appallingly high accident rate – the cost in a single year was computed at £19 million. The staff officers consisted of an Air Commodore, two Group Captains and 12 Squadron Leaders. I would be visiting every overseas airfield where the RAF had refuelling or servicing personnel, carrying exhibits to demonstrate how accidents happened - engines, airframes, damaged propellers. We carried them in a Dakota, a large transport plane which had been converted for carrying stretchers for ambulance work, and we used the stretchers to display the exhibits, which was a convenient solution as they could easily be stored back in the aircraft when not in use.

As the lecturer in charge, I would give a 20-minute lecture to all the personnel on the base, pointing out how much the accidents cost each year and explaining with the aid of the exhibits how they had happened. The team also showed professionally-made cine film of simulated accidents. They had even filmed a real-life incident by locking down one wheel of a Mosquito to make it crash on the runway. We had to be very diplomatic dealing with the station commanders, who tended to see us as outsiders trying to snoop on their operations and find fault.

Here's one example of an accident which could easily have been prevented. An airman had been refuelling a Lancaster Bomber. In his pocket he had put a Ronson lighter, which was operated by a little spring-loaded lever. Having refuelled the aircraft he jumped down from the wing.

As he landed the lighter fell from his pocket and hit the ground, triggering the lever. Unfortunately, petrol fumes had escaped - there was a flash and a bang and the aircraft was engulfed in flames. It was completely destroyed.

We gave them a simple solution to this one – never carry lighters or matches of any description when working on an aircraft.

We left RAF Manston at the start of September 1947 and headed for our first station, an RAF base near Bordeaux. From Bordeaux we went to Marseilles and from there along the east coast of Spain to Gibraltar. The aircraft were flown by specially-trained crews from the Communications Squadron at Hendon, each consisting of a pilot, second pilot, wireless operator and navigator. They flew VIPs, members of the Government and royalty, so they were trained to a very high standard. They would each do a three-month tour before being replaced by fresh crew.

From Gibraltar we flew along the North African coast, which I had last seen in 1943 during the invasion of Sicily. We gave our lecture at Algiers, Tunisia and Malta, where we visited two stations, including a naval training base at Hal Far, before flying on to Tripoli and El Adem in Libya.

I had often wondered what the officers really thought of our lectures, so I was interested to be told when we arrived in the Canal Zone that the Senior Air Staff Officer, a highly-decorated Air Commodore or Air Vice Marshall called McGhee, who was from New Zealand, and his staff at the RAF headquarters there wanted to see our show. At the end of the talk he called me to one side and said he was surprised at how valuable the lecture was and hoped we would meet with a friendly reception on all the RAF stations under his command. I think he had heard that we were regarded in some quarters as almost a 'Gestapo' unit which would make complaints about the way stations were run. Nothing could have been further from our minds.

From the Canal Zone we went to Khartoum and Aden, then to Nairobi and down into Rhodesia and South Africa. The South Africans greeted us warmly, and we were asked to deliver the lecture to some of their engineers at Calvin House in Johannesburg. Here the heat melted part of the projector, but the engineers managed to rustle up one of their own. They took me to visit the Rose Deep gold mine at Germiston, where I was taken a mile underground.

From South Africa we travelled to Bulawayo in Rhodesia, Tanganyika, Juba and Kenya, arriving back in Khartoum in October. Here we had a few days to spare. I was told that as RAF officers we had automatic membership of the Sudan Club there, which had excellent facilities for wining and dining.

The club also had a near-Olympic-sized swimming pool, and here a remarkable reunion took place. As I was swimming towards the steps, I bumped into another swimmer. When I turned to apologise, I saw that it was Tony Bethell, whom I had last seen in 1942 when I had briefed him on a sortie into Holland. As mentioned earlier, he was one of those who had survived the Great Escape of 1944.

On the airbase at Khartoum was a transit mess to accommodate officers and other senior civilian passengers travelling between Europe and South Africa or Rhodesia. Outside the entrance I saw a Sudanese trader who was selling ivory trinkets such as dolls and animals, cigarette boxes and jewellery cases. After some haggling I bought a small, intricately-carved jewellery box.

The trader was a tall, fine-looking Sudanese, dressed in a long, white garment which was covered by a long, well-tailored cotton jacket which reached almost to his ankles. He had three tribal marks carved on each cheek, and his turban was immaculately laundered.

Having made my purchase, we got chatting. He introduced himself as Moustafa Farahat. He said that when he left his stall to pray he would leave his wares unattended, and I asked him if he was afraid that they would be stolen. He replied that he had been leaving them there for up to an hour and a half every day for more than two years, and none had ever been stolen. He had great faith in the British. He then invited me and my deputy, Squadron Leader Peter Alt, to visit him at his home in Omdurman, across the river from Khartoum. We thanked him and said we would try to come the next morning.

Just after midday the following day, I was called to the telephone to find Moustafa on the line. He said he appreciated that we might be having difficulty getting a taxi out to Omdurman, so he was ordering a taxi for us. Sure enough, about an hour later, a taxi turned up. It drove us to a house down a very narrow street, and we were met at a door in the wall by our trader, who ushered us into a tidy little courtyard. Here he introduced us to his six sons, who appeared to be aged from about 22 to no more than four. They were lined up in order of height, from the tallest on the right to the smallest on the left. They made a fine body of young men, all elegantly turned out in freshly-laundered white clothes and turbans.

We sat on chairs and talked. On my left sat Moustafa's father, who, we were told, was a camel and cattle trader. We could hear our host's two wives chattering away loudly, although we never caught a glimpse of them. He had told me previously that one was black and the other was white – I think he meant that one was black and the other was less black. We were treated to sherbet and a large tin of Sharp's Creamy Toffees.

That night we were able to entertain Tony Bethell to dinner in the Sudan Club before setting off the following day for the eight-hour journey back to the Canal Zone. Here we gave more lectures before setting off to Palestine and then eventually on to Habbaniya in Iraq. From Habbaniya we visited Shaibah, an isolated RAF station not far from Basra at the head of the Gulf, and then Bahrain. We refuelled at a little desert station on the edge of the Gulf before proceeding on the long flight to Karachi in Pakistan.

Chapter 12

It was the middle of November when we arrived at Mauripur, the RAF station at Karachi. This was three months after Pakistan and India had gained independence. We were greeted warmly enough, but the Pakistanis were already in full charge of the station and enforcing the customs and health regulations which governed entry. As it happens I had had my yellow fever inoculation in the native hospital in Bulawayo - I still have the certificate among my papers - so I was let into Pakistan without any trouble. However Squadron Leader Alt and the wireless operator had both had theirs signed in South Africa, and the Pakistani doctors would not recognise a South African certificate because of apartheid. As a result, both men were immediately put in quarantine for ten days.

When I was told the Pakistani officials had taken my colleagues away, I went outside to see a little van which was covered in perforated zinc, like a meat safe. Inside were Peter Alt and the wireless operator. They were driven off and incarcerated in a large building on the outskirts of Karachi, along with a number of Pakistani Muslims returning from Mecca.

When they were finally released, the two men said they had been kept in an awful place, and they had been concerned that some of the Pakistanis might infect them with tuberculosis. The officiousness of the Pakistanis was making a difficult situation very much worse. I felt it was an indication of what was to come now that the British were no longer in charge.

We flew on to a number of Indian stations, including Jaipur, where we met the Maharajah and his wife. We flew from Delhi back into Pakistan, and at Peshawar we met a Pakistani officer who said he would look after us. On the way to Peshawar, at an altitude of 12,000 feet, we could see the Himalayas reaching up into the sky; a magnificent sight.

On reaching Peshawar I bumped into Peter Morris, a former member of No.268 Squadron, who was now a Squadron Leader on loan to the Pakistani Air Force. He was in charge of their Air Observation Post Squadron, which flew the small Auster passenger aircraft. They had watched the exchange of populations as independence was declared on August 15, when the Muslims in India had tried to reach Pakistan and the Indians in Pakistan had tried to reach the safety of India. Both sides were responsible for stopping trains carrying people across the border, and Peter told me he had seen at least a million people lying dead by the side of the railway tracks.

Apart from these horrors, Peter seemed to be enjoying his service with the Pakistani forces. He lived in a bungalow with a large garden and had several servants, including a nurse to look after his children, a cook, a housemaid, gardeners and a guard at the front door overnight.

Peter arranged for me to have a day's hunting. He was a member of the Peshawar Vale Hunt, established by the British in 1870; pictures of some of the former masters were on view in the club in the cantonment (a large army base), which stood in a tree-lined avenue close to the airfield. My host was about the same build as me, so he was able to fix me up with breeches, riding boots and a topee (a sun hat). We were driven to the meet for a 7 am start – hunting would be over by midday because of the heat, even in November.

The hunt was now controlled by a Pakistani Lieutenant Colonel, but it was still being run very much like the Bicester hunt I knew so well. In fact the hounds were the spitting image of our Bicester hounds - black, white and tan, and the same size. The hunt had been started with some bitches taken out by officers serving with the Indian Army, while dog hounds were taken out every two or three years to introduce fresh blood.

I had a wonderful day's hunting. The hounds normally hunted jackals, but occasionally they sighted foxes which had come down from the Himalayas. We found jackals in small clumps of sugar cane and small plantations of wheat which were growing among the grassland to the north of Peshawar. There were no hedges to be jumped, but we had to jump many narrow waterways. The horse I was riding, a charger which had been the property of General Gracie when he was commanding one of the armies in Burma, had been well trained to get across them. He would stop at the edge of the stream and cat-jump to the other side.

At noon, with the sun getting high and the heat extreme, the Master called it a day and we went home. Apart from the heat, it was very much like a foxhunt conducted back home at Bicester. The turnout and the way the hunt was conducted were first rate.

Over the few days I was there I was given the services of a 16-year-old Pakistani youth who was smartly turned out in a turban with a red, white and blue ribbon round the edge. He was delighted to work for a British officer again, as he hadn't been employed since the British had left some weeks before. He told me he was expecting to marry within a few weeks. He had never seen his future wife, who was just 12 years old.

I told him that I would soon be going off to Australia and asked if he knew where that was on the map. He had been at the British school organised in the cantonment under the Indian government, and his education seemed to be reasonable. He did indeed know where Australia was, and said he would like to accompany me there if that was possible, and if necessary he would be delighted to come to England with me, in spite of the fact that he was betrothed.

We spent a day visiting Risalpur, another Pakistani station about 50 miles away, where once again we were well received. We then crossed back into India to visit two more Indian stations before flying down to Bombay and on to Ceylon, where we landed on the southern tip of the island on a small airfield called Koggalla.

The airfield at Koggalla consisted of a concrete runway with the sea at one end and a lake at the other. The lake was only a few feet deep, just enough to take a Sunderland flying boat, of which there were three. We were told they were likely to remain there for some weeks while the Air Ministry decided what to do with them. They were expensive aircraft to fly, but they were useful for communication between India, Singapore and Australia. They always returned from their Australian trips with plenty of food, groceries and other requirements needed by RAF personnel stationed there.

We spent Christmas day 1947 on this little outpost, and enjoyed an excellent Christmas dinner of turkey which had been flown in from Australia.

After Christmas we took off for Madras and then Calcutta. We stayed only one night in Calcutta, where it was depressing to see people sleeping in the streets. Many appeared to be very hungry, as there was a shortage of food in that part of India.

We took off from Calcutta to land at an airfield near Rangoon, and from there we flew to Malaya and landed at Butterworth, an air base opposite Penang Island. Having refuelled at Butterworth, we flew on to Singapore, landing at Changi. We gave lectures at three airport stations in Singapore before leaving for the long flight to Australia.

Just before we left, we were told to divert to Hong Kong to put on our exhibition at Kai Tak airfield, on the mainland opposite Hong Kong island. We flew there via Saigon, a dangerous place even then. The French had very little control over it. There was a 7 pm curfew, so we did not dare to venture out to visit any of the nightclubs.

We stayed in Hong Kong for a few days and were able to see a good deal of the island. Then we left for Australia. We had to refuel first at Sourabaya in Java, and then in Dutch Timor, where we had to refuel from four-gallon cans. It was a little airfield on the west of the island with very few facilities, and was really only there for use in an emergency by RAF aircraft making the long crossing from Singapore to Darwin.

In Darwin, the Australians seemed rather casual about our lecture. However we were better received when we reached Melbourne and met some senior Royal Australian Air Force officers. We were interviewed by the Australian Broadcasting Company.

Chapter 12

After the food rationing back in Europe, Australia was a revelation. Huge quantities of meat were available in the hotels, not because the Australians wanted to keep the food for themselves but because the shipping wasn't available to take it anywhere else.

We visited Adelaide, Sydney, Wagga-Wagga, Newcastle and finally an airfield near Brisbane. In Sydney, we were treated to a day at the races and found that the Australians were great racing and bloodstock enthusiasts.

We spent one weekend at an excellent hotel in Surfers' Paradise. The evening we arrived there we got drinking with an Australian and although the bar shut at 9 pm, we had all consumed a considerable quantity of beer, particularly the Australian, by the time we got to bed. At breakfast the next morning we managed a normal English breakfast of cereal, fruit and bacon and eggs, but the Australian devoured an enormous steak topped with a fried egg.

While in Sydney I took time off to visit my wife's uncle, who had settled there after the First World War. He had felt so fit while serving in the hot climate of Egypt that he decided to leave the fogs and mists of Buckinghamshire and try his luck as a farmer in Australia. He hadn't been very successful as a farmer, but had instead ended up looking after a privately-owned zoo in Parramatta, outside Sydney which had lots of koala bears and other Australian animals. He had never been back to England and although his children and grandchildren did eventually pay the UK a visit, he himself never revisited the country of his birth.

Queensland was the last call on our lecture tour. All we had to look forward to now was the long journey back to the UK. We went back via the same stops - Darwin, Java, Singapore, Rangoon, Calcutta, Delhi, Karachi, the Persian Gulf stations, Iraq, the Egyptian Canal Zone, and home via the south of France. By the time we touched down at Bassingbourne, Cambridge, it was March 18 1948.

For the rest of that year I continued with my accident prevention role, though now back on more familiar soil.

Chapter 13

Back in the UK
1949-1951

My next posting was more down to earth. I was posted as Commanding Officer at RAF Woodvale, a large airfield near Southport, Lancashire, which was the home of the Liverpool University Air Squadron. It was well drained with good approaches and made an ideal training airfield for the undergraduates. The officers' mess was a wooden hut, as were most of the airfield buildings, while a row of small brick houses housed a few families of those serving at the station.

The adjutant was a Flight Lieutenant and there were three excellent flying instructors.

In Southport there were excellent facilities for tennis, swimming and entertainment of all kinds, and we even had a squash court.

The station was easy to run and problems were very few. However it seemed that some of the wives of the airmen had complaints to air, so I organised a fortnightly meeting with them with tea, coffee, sandwiches and cakes. This seemed to work very well; the airmen and their wives were delighted to have the chance to meet the CO over a cup of tea on more or less level terms.

It was while I was at Woodvale that we were hit by the Liverpool dock strikes, which brought the docks to a standstill. After some days the Labour Government realised that they could not afford to have food ships lying idle in the docks with people on short rations and barely getting enough to eat, and decided to employ servicemen to unload the ships. This meant accommodating a large number of airmen and soldiers at Woodvale, and I received instructions from Air Ministry to make our hangar available to accommodate up to 2000 men.

Chapter 13

We removed the aircraft from the hangar and made arrangements to bring in palliasses on which the airmen and soldiers working at the docks would sleep. One of our airmen then pointed out that hundreds, if not thousands, of beds were now being handed in at No. 15 Maintenance Unit in Lancashire as a result of all the closures of RAF stations, and asked if we could use them, so that was exactly what we did.

The Government was concerned that troublemakers might try to stir up feeling against the servicemen, so we were instructed to make their stay as comfortable as possible. A mobile cinema was brought in for entertainment and high-quality meals were laid on. After a few days the Trade Unionists realised the food ships were going to be unloaded whether they liked it or not and decided to go back to work.

It was a satisfactory ending to a very delicate situation, and I received a special commendation from whoever was in charge of the operation at the Air Ministry for the cooperation I had shown. Then, a few weeks after the strike had ended, I received notice that I was to be posted to the RAF Selection Boards. As the post involved was that of Wing Commander, it appeared I was in line for a further promotion. I was very grateful to the airman who had suggested the bed idea.

Before joining the Boards in July 1949 I undertook a 14-day personnel selection course at RAF Hornchurch. I found this very useful. It gave me an understanding of managing people which I found valuable for the rest of my service career, and indeed in my peacetime activities.

At the end of the course I reported to the Selection Board offices at Alexander House in Kingsway. There were four boards, each typically made up of a Wing Commander and two Squadron Leaders. When applicants to the educational or engineering branch were being interviewed, an additional member joined from that branch.

Every effort was made to put the candidates at ease. Each man was first given an informal interview with a single officer to gather information about him, which was then passed to the boards before the interview.

The two years that followed with the Selection Boards was a very comfortable time. I was able to return to the farm each weekend to give a hand with the work there.

One day I was sitting on a Board when who should come before me but John Nesbitt Dufour, who had been my flying instructor when I first joined for pilot training. He later became a most successful Lysander pilot taking agents across the Channel and picking them up from various locations deep inside France. He had applied to come back in as an instructor. I did not think it right to reveal all I knew about his activities.

Because I worked in the Department of Personnel, it was fairly easy to arrange for the sort of posting I wanted. By now I was feeling an urge to return to flying, so in the autumn of 1951 I asked for the opportunity to go on a one-month pilot refresher course including the Instrument Flying Course, which qualified the pilot for a Green Ticket.

The Green Ticket was a card authorising the holder to operate or fly in almost any weather conditions. It was the cardholder's responsibility to assess the conditions and decide whether he was able to cope with them. It was arranged for me to attend the course at Newton on the banks of the River Trent. This was an airfield which was easy to find in murky weather conditions because it was right on the river.

The course started in early November, to give us a good chance of encountering the low cloud, rain, mist, frost and snow which we had to learn to deal with. Everything went very well and I was pleased when the course finished and I was assessed as above average.

I was not much impressed, however, by my first instructor – in fact I was able to teach him a thing or two. He admitted that I had shown him how to improve his stall turns. After about ten days I was allocated a new instructor, a Flight Lieutenant who had joined the RAF after escaping from Czechoslovakia just before the war. He was a first-class pilot and a first-class instructor. I was lucky to have him - he certainly improved my flying ability.

Chapter 13

Those on the course were mainly middle-ranking officers such as Wing Commanders or Squadron Leaders, but there were also two Group Captains. They were both delightful chaps. I remember them happily playing darts in the officers' mess, which was unusual, to say the least.

One of the Group Captains was the Air Attaché from Denmark. He left the course early, as he seemed to feel a couple of outings in a Meteor were all he needed. Shortly after he went back, I read that he had been killed in an air crash. I never found out what exactly caused his accident, but it may have been the lack of refresher training or conversion training to jet aircraft – though jets were usually much easier to fly than propeller-driven aircraft.

The other Group Captain was Sam Ellworthy, a bomber pilot from New Zealand with an excellent record. I remember him saying that after the war all the top posts were being taken by pilots who had fought in the Battle of Britain, as if they were the only people that counted, while the more dangerous work done by Bomber Command and Coastal Command was overlooked. He pointed out that all the station commanders in Germany at that time were Battle of Britain men, as were the Wing Commanders flying on the German stations. The Senior Air Staff Officer at the headquarters of the British Air Forces of Occupation was Air Vice Marshall Sir Harry Broadhurst, who had been a wing leader and later a Group Captain during the Battle of Britain.

It's true that those who had fought in the Battle of Britain milked their status for all it was worth. Even today, when someone who fought in the Battle of Britain dies, you can guarantee that the survivors will flock to his funeral.

When Sam Ellworthy reached a more senior position in the Air Ministry things did start to change, and by late 1951 more Bomber Command and Coastal Command men were being considered for promotion. Ellworthy later became Air Chief Marshall, and just before his retirement he reached the highest rank in the RAF - Marshall of the

Royal Air Force, equivalent to Field Marshall. After he retired I believe he had a distinguished post at Windsor Castle and was elevated to the House of Lords.

I did feel a bomber pilot needed greater reserves of courage and fortitude than the fighter pilots in the Battle of Britain. Imagine a pilot on a mission to bomb Berlin. For the last 15 minutes of his approach he'd be flying into a cauldron of flak, with seven men behind him relying on his courage and skill.

Not surprisingly, we had a problem called 'creepback'. Instead of hanging on grimly and getting all the way to the target, there was a great temptation for some pilots to drop their loads perhaps five miles short and hurry back home. The next man, seeing where the first bombs had struck, would drop his bombs six miles short, and so on until some of the bombs were falling 20 miles short of the target. The only answer was to fit all the bombers with cameras to record the bomb bursts on the ground and make sure they were reaching the target.

Most of those who completed a bombing tour of 30 missions were awarded with a DFC or DFM. If they didn't get that or a Mention in Despatches, it was probably because the photos had shown that their bombs were not near enough to the targets.

Another of the officers on the course was Wing Commander Piers Kelly, who had been my Flight Commander in 1939 when I had joined No.4 Squadron. In July 1939 he had been posted to the Embassy in Paris because he was a fluent French speaker. Now that I had been promoted to Wing Commander, I had caught up with him.

My logbook shows that I put in 23 hours 15 minutes dual flying on my refresher course and 21 hours 45 minutes solo, with 14 hours 30 minutes instrument flying. The final test, flying blind for 65-70 minutes, was very difficult, but it was a course I'd always wanted to do and I was very gratified to pass because a lot of officers of my seniority hadn't yet undertaken it. Passing the test meant that I was given a "green ticket", authorising me to make my own judgements about flying in any conditions without having to go to a higher authority.

At the completion of the course, we were all transferred to the jet conversion course at RAF Middleton St George. We were only there for a couple of days before we were sent on Christmas leave. On my return I received instructions to report to Number 2 Group headquarters in Gütersloh, Germany. I was somewhat reluctant to go, as Daphne was pregnant and had contracted a severe case of German measles, but I had little choice.

Little did I know that as far as my RAF career was concerned, this was to be the last

Chapter 14

Last posting
RAF Fassberg, 1952

On arrival at RAF G_tersloh I reported to the senior personnel Staff Officer, who introduced me to the Air Officer Commanding, Air Commodore Hector McGregor. He welcomed me to the group and told me that the next day I was to proceed to RAF Fassberg, where I would be taking up flying duties under Group Captain Donaldson. I knew Donaldson – I had last seen him in the bar of the Surrey pub on the Strand in June 1944, when he had just returned from instructing the Americans in the fighter tactics which had been so successful during the Battle of Britain.

I arrived at Fassberg late the following afternoon, in deep snow. I was met at the railway station by Group Captain Donaldson and Wing Commander Johnny Johnson, his Wing Commander Flying, who drove me to the base. I knew Johnson too, as we had met several times in the RAF Officers' Club in Brussels in the winter of 1944/45.

When we got to the officers' mess at RAF Fassberg, Donaldson invited me to take a drink with him before dinner. I excused myself by saying that I had been travelling all day and would rather freshen up in my room.

"I hope you're not a teetotaller" he said. "We had a couple of officers posted to us a few days ago who were both teetotallers. It'll be a dull place if all the officers are like that."

That evening I met most of the pilots and Squadron Leaders of the three squadrons which constituted the Wing at RAF Fassberg. The next morning I reported for duty at the airfield, where I met the rest of the pilots. No flying was possible because of the heavy snow, and all available personnel were employed on clearing the runway.

This was a tedious operation, and a special tool had been designed to speed up the process. It consisted of a six-foot broom handle, at the end of which was attached a lightweight board about two feet square with which you would push the snow from the centre of the runway to the edge. Unfortunately this had built up a large ridge of snow on either side of the runway, which had grown to about two feet high and frozen solid. It created a serious hazard for any aircraft which might slide into it.

Almost everyone on the station was employed in keeping the runway free of snow. The only personnel who escaped were the cooks, who were busy preparing hot food and drinks for the rest of us.

I was able to have long talks with the squadron commanders, particularly Squadron Leader Sutherland, who was very helpful in keeping me up to date with all the operational requirements with the Vampire Fighter squadrons with which the Second Tactical Air Force was equipped. The De Havilland Vampire, with a single jet engine, was a very easy aircraft to fly, although its air speed and rate of climb were not much better than the Spitfire.

Not long after I arrived at Fassberg, Donaldson invited me to be present while he interviewed two young officers who had been caught in the red light district of Hamburg, which was of course out-of-bounds to all officers. He berated these men for a full ten minutes, threatening them with all sorts of disciplinary action. I felt that all that was needed was a severe warning that if they offended again it could lead to court martial and demotion, or even their expulsion from the RAF.

A week or so after my arrival, Donaldson invited me to dinner at his house on the station. He and his wife had been allocated a large, comfortable, well-designed house built by the Germans for their middle-ranking officers before the war. His wife was an American girl whom he had met while serving with the American Air Force in United States. As the evening progressed I became aware that their marriage was under strain. They were speaking very sharply and acidly towards one another, which made the dinner rather uncomfortable for me.

After dinner it became clear that Donaldson was trying to find out more about me. He was astonished to learn that I had been a reconnaissance pilot rather than a fighter pilot.

It seemed he had taken his Squadron, No.151, to an airfield near Lille soon after the start of the Battle of France, so he was particularly interested in my stay in France in 1939-40. His Squadron must have moved to the French airfield on May 12 or 13 1940, after the Germans had crossed the frontier into Belgium.

I told Donaldson that we too had been near Lille, at Lille Marque, where we had given new pilots practice on the Lysander. I also told him how two of them had been shot down by German fighters which had made fast, low-level attacks from their bases in Germany. One of the men we had lost was Pilot Officer Butterworth, a Middlesex cricketer, while another was Pilot Officer Oldacres, from the West Country. They had joined the Squadron only the day before, so they had both been shot down and killed within 24 hours of arriving in France.

I told Donaldson that we could have done with some fighter protection at the time, as our Lysanders were easy meat to the Messerschmidts, which were almost twice as fast. We had been concerned that when our aircraft were shot down, the Hurricanes were still on the ground.

Donaldson now became rather uneasy. Some of his aircraft, of course, could have been on the airfield at the time. I realised that I might have inadvertently criticised his Squadron, and it had not gone down well.

Since I had arrived at Fassberg immediately after Christmas, I was soon caught up in the New Year festivities. Individual officers were throwing parties in their own married quarters, and there seemed to be a bash every night. Lots of alcohol was consumed. On Saturday evenings there was a dance in the officers' mess to which wives and girlfriends were invited. The younger officers would invite local nurses from the military hospitals which had been established after the war in northern Germany, or female officers from the joint Headquarters at G_tersloh or even Brussels.

One evening, Group Captain Donaldson told me that he wanted me to remain within his circle during the Saturday night events. I thought this was a most unusual request, as I had already used the dances as opportunities to talk to many of the other officers. Nevertheless I agreed, and each Saturday night I stayed with Donaldson and his acolytes. This seemed to work very well.

Unfortunately Donaldson liked to use me as the butt of his jokes, which often referred to my farming background. He obviously thought all farmers were rather slow-witted people. I pointed out that one of the most successful pilots of the Battle of Britain was a farmer's son from Shropshire by the name of Eric Locke, who had been awarded a DSO and DFC & Bar before being shot down and badly burned over South East England. After his burns had been treated he had returned to operational duty. Locke was finally shot down and killed over France while attacking ground targets.

In my third week at Fassberg I had to attend the 7th Armoured Division study week, which was held in a large theatre near L_neburg. I found it most interesting to be once again among middle-ranking and senior Army officers who had fought the key battles of the war, particularly the advance from the Normandy beachhead to Arnhem in September 1944 and the Battle of the Reichwald and the Crossing of the Rhine in March 1945.

At the end of the study week, I was still concerned about the health of my wife. I asked Group Captain Donaldson if he would allow me to return to England by air, taking one of the small aircraft, to visit her. At first he agreed. Then a couple of days later he told me that he and his wife were going off on leave – to a Swiss ski resort, I think - so I could not go after all, even though they were not due to go for another seven days.

By now the weather had improved, the snow had cleared and we were able to get on with normal training. I had not been able to fly since joining the wing, so I had asked the armament officer to put me on the training programme for the air-to-ground rocket firing which was due to start in a couple of days' time. This involved attacking an old tank placed in a sparsely-wooded area a few miles from the airfield. Our rockets would be observed from two positions, so the accuracy of their hits could be assessed.

Just before the programme started, I was approached by the Wing Commander in charge of the RAF Regiment Training Squadron, which was based on the airfield, and asked to supply two aircraft to carry out simulated low-flying attacks against the personnel under training. They would be dug-in in defensive positions on the training ground adjacent to the airfield.

I briefed Squadron Leader Sutherland, who had been most helpful to me, to carry out these attacks, as he had done it many times before and knew exactly what was required. I warned him not to fly below 200 feet. As I watched Sutherland's aircraft make the attacks from my office window later that morning, I thought they were going extremely well and the aircraft were just at the right height. They would come upon their targets unexpectedly, which was what the Wing Commander wanted.

As I was watching the exercise, the door of my office was suddenly flung open and I turned to see Group Captain Donaldson and a man in civilian clothes. "What the hell is going on?" barked Donaldson. "Do you know what you're doing? Are you mad allowing this low flying? Tell that pilot to land immediately!"

I got on the R/T and ordered Squadron Leader Sutherland to land immediately and report to my office. I then turned to Donaldson and explained that Sutherland had been carrying out attacks as required on the defensive positions which had been taken up by the RAF Regiment Training Squadron.

I imagined the civilian was the German clerk of works who sometimes accompanied the senior officer on a tour of inspection. I was most concerned to discover that he was in fact a Major Richardson, an officer junior to myself. Donaldson had been guilty of a major crime - admonishing an officer in the presence of a junior. This is an unforgivable sin in all the armed forces. In any case a senior officer should never shelter behind his rank in berating a subordinate, knowing that the junior officer cannot answer back. It is very much worse when the remarks are made in the presence of an officer who is junior to both.

I asked the Group Captain to stay until Squadron Leader Sutherland had reported to me to explain exactly the height at which he had been flying. We would also get a report from the Wing Commander in charge of the RAF Regiment Training Squadron as to whether he thought Sutherland had been flying lower than was required. But Donaldson said he had other parts of the station to visit, and he left before Sutherland got to my office.

Later that night, I was drinking in the mess with a group of young officers when Donaldson looked in. After staying a few minutes he told the bar steward: "I'm leaving now, when these young fellows have finished their drinks please close the bar". Then he left the room. Less than five minutes later he returned, obviously angry. He pointedly stood by me and said to the barman "I thought I had told you to close the bar?"

Such behaviour was most unusual in an RAF officers' mess. It was usual to leave the bar to the senior officer present, who would be responsible for maintaining law and order and finally closing the bar.

I was so incensed that when I got back to my room I wrote a full account of what had happened, clearly explaining that I had not authorised dangerous low flying, as Donaldson had implied when he had rushed into my office. At the end of it I pointed out that his rebuke had been at the very least ungentlemanly, and at most a breach of the accepted etiquette between officers. I thought I might get some kind of apology.

Earlier that day, the Group Captain had told me that I could not return to the UK to visit my sick wife, because he was going on leave. When, the following day, I had still not heard from him on either matter, I wrote a formal letter requesting that I should be allowed to resign my commission.

Having written the letter, I telephoned Donaldson in his office and asked to see him. He agreed. Before his adjutant showed me in, he assured me that he had given Donaldson the message I had left with him the previous morning, giving him advance notice of the planned training attacks.

I think Donaldson realised that I was resentful of his actions, because he now went out of his way to be pleasant, offering me coffee or tea. I suggested that he should read my letter before we did any socializing, and handed it to him. He did so, and I could see that he was shocked.

"I'm not going to forward this to a higher authority" he said.

"In that case sir, I must ask you to allow me to forward a copy of that letter to Group Headquarters for onward transmission to the Air Ministry" I replied. It was an embarrassing situation for him, and he forgot even to serve me the coffee he had ordered. After a few words of what he considered to be an explanation of what had happened the previous day, I was allowed to leave.

My letter of resignation had clearly made an impression. Donaldson now said I was free to return to the UK in a couple of days' time, and told me to leave the next day for group headquarters, where I would be interviewed by Air Commodore McGregor. The next day I packed my belongings and left by train. I didn't get to Group HQ until the late afternoon, and the Air Commodore was not able to see me until the next morning.

Air Commodore McGregor, a New Zealander, had been a Squadron Commander during the Battle of Britain. Like all such Squadron Commanders he had been awarded the DSO. He was typical of the New Zealanders with whom I had served; they always seemed more British than the British. Nevertheless he had little sympathy with my actions, or with the decision I had made to leave the service if I did not get an apology from Donaldson. He told me that he had great respect for all his Station Commanders and Group Captains, and held them in the highest regard.

I couldn't let pass the fact that Group Captain Tom Dalton-Morgan had recently been promoted to his rank on the recommendation of the Air Commodore, and that ten days later he had been exposed as a bigamist. He had married a young lady early in the war, then left her to marry another woman, with whom he was living in married quarters in Germany. One day his first wife had knocked on the door, to be met by the second Mrs Dalton-Morgan. So I took some satisfaction in remarking to Air Commodore McGregor that not all his station commanders were of the highest integrity. That only served to enrage him, and he ordered me to take a train back to England as soon as the SPSO (Senior Personnel Staff Officer) could arrange it.

I left the next day. Because of my wife's illness I had asked to be transported by air, which would have saved a day's travelling, but I was denied a place in the aircraft which made the daily return trip to the UK. When I did finally get home it was a great relief to see that Daphne was bearing up rather better than I had expected.

Just before I left Germany, a Senior Air Staff Officer called me in and told me that after I had spent some time with my wife I was to report to RAF Old Sarum to attend the Senior Officers' Course at the School of Land/Air Warfare. After making arrangements for Daphne to go into hospital, I signalled Group Headquarters in Germany asking that I should be given extended leave. I received no reply. When I called Old Sarum, I found that the signal had been received there but had not been sent on to me.

The Adjutant at Old Sarum suggested I should hold on until I received further instructions from my Group Headquarters in Germany, and said he would do all he could to help me to retain contact with my old unit.

He proved to be very kind, at a time when other people were being rather less helpful.

My enforced holiday did have some benefits. I was able to spend the next three weeks at home and take on some ploughing and other urgent farm work.

During my two years with the Selection Boards, the nine-to-five, five-days-a-week régime had allowed me to go home every Friday night and get a good deal of farm work done over the weekends before returning to London on the 6.45 am train on Monday morning. During that spring and early summer of 1951 it also gave me the chance to get up at four o'clock in the morning to do some of the lighter farm work, such as spraying pyrethrum powder against the turnip fly when it attacked the tiny seedlings of kale. The powder had to be applied in the still air of dawn.

I was hoping Mr Collett might sell me another 50 acres before long, as he was thinking of retiring and had no son to take over the farm. If I was going to leave, this was the time to do it. By leaving after 14 years' service, I would forfeit the pension I would have been entitled to after 15 years, but I was prepared to do so because I felt that in the long term my family would be better off if I went back to farming. The pension of course would end with my death, whereas the farm would create an ongoing income.

After three weeks at home, I received a letter from the Air Ministry telling me to report to Adastral House to meet a Group Captain to discuss my further employment. When I reported there the officer asked me where I would like to be posted to. I saw that he had on his file my letter asking to leave the service, along with a letter Donaldson had written to Air Commodore McGregor explaining why he thought Squadron Leader Sutherland had been guilty of unauthorised low flying, and why he had spoken to me in the office so coarsely.

I told the officer that I was not inclined to change my decision and that I still wished to leave the RAF because of the treatment I had received at the hands of Group Captain Donaldson. He said he thought I was being foolhardy, but promised to pass on my comments to a senior officer.

I then received another letter from the Air Ministry, inviting me to an interview with yet another Group Captain. This one offered me a variety of posts, all overseas. They did include some excellent flying jobs, one of which was in the Canal Zone. I should have liked to have taken that one on, as Group Captain Anderson was still commanding a station out there. But I decided to stick to my guns. The Group Captain gave me his best wishes, and I left.

It was early May 1952 when I received my next Air Ministry letter. This one invited me to an interview with Air Vice-Marshall Allinson, who held a top job in the Department of Personnel. He received me with great courtesy and understanding, and said he could arrange for my posting to any type of duty I liked. He asked me if there were any other reasons for my wanting to leave the RAF, and if the pay was perhaps not enough.

I replied that if I was being paid to fly, I was actually being overpaid, because it was something I had always wanted to do.

"You have an unblemished 14-year record - why throw it away?" Allinson asked me. "You will lose the opportunity of a significant pension after 20 years." But six more years seemed a long time to wait, and I was worried about what would happen to the farm in the meantime. My father was approaching his mid seventies and was able to do less work. Running the farm had become quite a burden to him and my mother.

There was a further reason for leaving. I told Allinson: "I have been married for ten years, and my wife and I have never been able to have RAF accommodation on a station, so in effect we have been separated all that time, with only visits at weekends." He replied that he could find me married quarters the next day.

I felt very sad about it all, but having weighed everything up, I knew I had to press ahead with my decision to leave the service. Allinson wished me the best of luck, and I saluted smartly and left his office.

That was the end of my time with the Royal Air Force. I had enjoyed every minute of it. I had revelled in the comradeship, the experience and the opportunities to travel. I had actually managed to visit every overseas RAF station.

Finally I had a letter from the Air Member for Personnel, an official document thanking me for my services to the RAF and stating that I would now go on to the retired list and be available for recall up to the age of 60.

My clash with Donaldson did not have much effect on his subsequent career. He did of course already have an excellent history in the RAF, having led the aerobatic team which had become World Champions at the International Show in Switzerland before the war - he had been awarded the Air Force Cross for that. He had led a flight of three Gladiators performing the most intricate aerobatics, with three aircraft joined together by rubber ropes. For a couple of years after the war he also held the world flying speed record, at 616 miles an hour, in a Meteor jet. He stayed on in the RAF, gaining a CBE and eventually a CB. If he had risen one more rank, to Air Vice Marshal, he would probably have been knighted.

After Donaldson retired he got a highly-paid job as air correspondent for the Daily Telegraph. When he died at the age of about 80, I went to his funeral, out of curiosity rather than respect, which was held in the little church at Tangmere. In that churchyard lie a number of former Battle of Britain pilots who had no strong affiliations with churches in their own towns or villages, so they elected to be buried there, close to the airfield from which they had flown during the Battle of Britain.

The only family mourner appeared to be the daughter of his first marriage, who was clearly proud of what her father had achieved. To me, however, he will always be a bully who took advantage of his rank to shield himself from retaliation from a junior officer.

Chapter 15

Back to the farm
1952-59

When I finally got back home for good in February 1952, I knew I had a lot of work to do to bring in a living wage and ensure a reasonably comfortable life for me and my growing family. I didn't want to take any of my father's earnings from the farm, as it was barely producing enough profit for my parents to live on.

Fortunately they still had an income from the property my father had inherited from my grandmother. Some of the houses had been destroyed in the Blitz, but he still had about 25 houses in Moray Road. Some of the smaller ones were still let at the rents that had been set when they were built 40 years earlier, which in some cases was as little as £2 a week. Many of the larger houses were sublet.

Bert MacFarlane, my father's cousin, had been administering the estate, but at the age of 75 he decided to give this up and implement the terms of my grandmother's will, which provided for the properties to be divided into three lots. One lot was to go to my father, one to Aunt Dora Prince and the other to the daughters of my aunt, Nelly Berry. Aunt Nelly had died in 1930, so her share went to her daughters, Mary, Muriel and Margaret.

My first act on taking up the reins of the farm once again was to order 300 day-old chicks. I planned to rear 250 of these in laying cages and use the rest as free-range birds for the Christmas trade. I employed two bricklayers, Bert Castle and John "Dolly" Holloway, to repair the old chicken house my grandfather had built in 1901.

I ordered the cages from a firm in Blackpool, and by September 1952 I had 240 pullets to put into them. I had reared the young hens under an electric lamp in a new chicken house which I had bought from a carpenter and wheelwright in Weston on the Green, and hardened them off on wheat and barley stubble on the land we had bought from Richard Collett.

All went well, and by October we were producing 150 eggs a day. They were collected by an eggler – the old term for an egg dealer – based in Waddesdon, who came every Monday. I was able to offset the rearing costs by feeding my hens on wheat produced on the farm, and I suggested to my father that this should be in lieu of the wages that I would have otherwise earned from it. He was happy with that.

As the months went by it became clear just how much work I was going to have to do on the farm to justify my decision to give up an RAF salary. We were going to have to greatly increase production. With the help of Dolly Holloway and Bert Castle, I converted the old stables into cow standings, while a small loosebox near the dairy held another five cows and a small shed at the end of the barn would take four more. This gave us about 30 cows to milk, and we were soon sending 100 gallons of milk away every day.

We also bought a second tractor, a little grey Ferguson, which enabled us to complete our cultivation much more quickly. By the end of 1952 I felt we had made a fair start in putting the business on a sound footing, small as it was.

Haymaking and harvesting were still a time-consuming operation, so we hired a baler from a local farmer. This captured my father's interest, and at the following year's Oxfordshire Agricultural Show he spent over £1000 on a new hay baler, a Salopian baler with an Armstrong-Siddeley engine, made by a firm in Shropshire and built under licence from an American firm.

The purchase astonished me, as he had not discussed the idea with me. It wasn't even the best baler on the market. The model everyone wanted was made by the International Harvester Company of America, but very few of these were available in England in 1953 and although there were one or two at the show, they had already been sold. Our baler required a lot of careful maintenance and there were frequent breakages, particularly with the needles which carried the string through the bale before the knots were tied and the bale discharged from the rear.

Nevertheless, we were able to keep our baler going all through the summer and autumn of 1953 and I was able to undertake a good deal of contract baling, first of hay and then straw. I had a contract with the manager of a farm at Wendlebury who was managing it on behalf of a Mr Drexler, a rich Jewish refugee from Czechoslovakia who owned an office equipment business in Aylesbury. He had an excellent young manager who wanted all the straw from his cereal crops to be baled. He used the barley straw for fodder and the wheat straw for bedding.

We had delightful weather for the harvesting in late August and early September 1953, and I was able to bale until two in the morning, thanks to some lights I had fitted to the tractor. They allowed me to illuminate the swathe so that I could see if it was being fed properly into the baler.

These were such beautiful nights that I could easily have slept on a blanket beside the baler, ready to start again as soon as the sun burned the dew off the straw the next morning. It made me think of the tank crews in Normandy in 1944, sleeping under blankets beside their tanks. During my RAF service I had always enjoyed sleeping under canvas and enjoyed many a refreshing night's sleep that way.

Nearly sixty years on, I was talking to a hard-working young farmer I know who uses a big £60,000 baler. I suggested he might consider sleeping by his baler on fine nights as I had once considered. He has an astonishing capacity for working long hours. Sometimes he works through the night, has a quick breakfast brought to him in the field, then carries on baling all through the next day, clocking up 36 hours without a break.

At the end of the harvest that year, I added up the income from all the contract work I had done and the bills I had sent out for my work and discovered that I had paid for the baler in its first year, along with the string and the diesel it consumed. I didn't count my time, otherwise it would have been a different picture, but it was gratifying to note just the same.

The first combine harvesters had come to England from the USA in 1943. Two were allocated to the Bicester area, and both were bought by members of the local Agricultural Committee. During the war, to buy machinery such as a tractor or combine harvester, you had to produce a Certificate of Need to prove that your farm was of a large enough acreage. If it wasn't, you were expected to do additional work for farmers who could not afford to buy one. My father had applied to buy a standard Fordson tractor at the beginning of the war, and was finally given the authority to do so just as the war finished.

In April 1954 our family increased again with the birth in April of another daughter, Jennifer. The same year I approached the Agriculture Advisor for Oxfordshire, a Mr Richards. He came along to take soil samples, which showed that our fertility was low. The soil was rich in lime and needed large quantities of phosphates, potash and nitrogen to maintain fertility and guarantee an economic return.

He suggested that on the drought-prone stone-brash soil of Hawkwell and Lords Farm, we should not stick to rye grasses. He recommended that we should try three varieties of cocksfoot which had been bred by the plant-breeding station at Aberystwyth in Wales, and plant them with white clover. Cocksfoots are not quite as palatable to cattle as rye grasses, but they grew well in our dry conditions and the clover made them more acceptable to the animals.

Our cattle seemed to thrive on this, and there was little difference in the milk yield. The hay too was less palatable than the rye grass hay, but the cattle never refused it and continued to thrive. We did try to give softer hay to the young calves.

We had stuck to the old four-course crop rotation which had been followed since my grandfather had introduced it at the turn of the century.

Chapter 15

In the early days he had maintained fertility with sheep, and we still had a breeding flock of Suffolk sheep which spent much of the year within hurdles and were folded (confined) on roots and kale in the winter.

In the autumn the ewes were often flushed (given extra rich feed) on young grasses or vetches in order to increase their rate of conception. When the sheep had been on vetches or roots, we always knew the corn crop that followed would be a good one. As a child of seven or eight I used to find it hard walking through a field of vetches, because my legs would get tangled up with the dense mat of plants.

Around 1954, Richard Collett came to see me to tell me that he was planning to sell another 50 acres, and wanted to give me first refusal. I was glad to accept his offer. We could now farm more land with the same machinery and labour, which increased our profits.

In about 1955 we bought a steerage hoe to mount on the rear of the little Ferguson, to hoe and weed our kale crops. We could now hoe four rows at a time, making the work much faster, easier and more effective. Things were so different from the days of my boyhood, when I would lead one horse while my father did the hoeing behind, a row at a time - it could take all day to hoe a single acre of kale. Now, with my father driving the tractor and me operating the steerage hoe, we could do ten acres in a day comfortably.

Neither of us had to do any walking. All my father had to do at the end of each row was lift the lever with his right hand to raise the hoe with me on it, turn the tractor and position it for the next row, then lower the hoe again. It was a very simple operation and my father loved it, even though he was now nearly 80. He used to come into my house in the morning and say "Come along Bill, finish your breakfast and let's get hoeing".

The increased kale production gave us more feed for the cows during the winter months. The hay blades in the middle of the rows pushed the soil towards the kale plants on either side and the L blade, if properly set, contributed to this, so the roots were in deeper soil and had access to more nutrients. The new method also kept the rows clear of weeds.

My father was of course concerned about the cost of the equipment. When I told him I was thinking of buying a new implement his usual reaction was to ask who was going to pay for it – despite the fact that he was earning the equivalent of a Squadron Leader's salary, while my earnings were barely at the level of a Flight Lieutenant. Very often I replied that I would pay for it myself, and would raid my small savings. It helped that I had the £2000 the Air Ministry had given me at the end of my service. But the tractor and hoe soon proved to be a sound investment, because our winter milk returns became significantly higher.

Unfortunately the summer of 1955 was a very wet one. It rained every day for six weeks, and much of the hay crop was so blackened that it had to be burned. We lost 25 acres of hay. That was a mistake - the weather changed in August and we had hot sun, so if we had waited we could have baled it and used it for bedding.

In 1954 we had seen the end of meat rationing, which led to a small drop in the value of agricultural produce. Many foods which had been rationed were suddenly in surplus. As rationing ended altogether competition became much greater and food prices started to fall. Retailers like Jack Cohen, who founded Tesco, were able to sell all sorts of commodities at low prices on the "pile them high, sell them cheap" principle.

Of course the consumer benefited, and standards of living started to rise. Housing was now much better too. In Bucknell we saw the demolition of tiny thatched cottages with small windows and low ceilings, which had no sewage system and no water supply other than a standpipe in the street. It was good to see these old insanitary houses pulled down and new council homes built in their stead.

The planners made a mistake in Bucknell, though. We had about an acre of green open space in the middle of the village, and they used it for the new council houses instead of leaving it as a village green. But the houses were of excellent quality, and perhaps it was wrong of those of us who would have liked to have seen a village green to suggest that the houses should have been tucked away somewhere else.

September 1956 saw the fifth addition to the family, when our second son, Tim, was born.

The late 1950s saw slow progress on the farm, with modest profits. We were helped by an unexpected windfall from the taxman. I had engaged an accountant, Mr Penfold, to look at my father's affairs and the farm accounts. Up till then, instead of producing annual accounts, we had been paying tax based on the acreage we farmed, which was usual in those days. Mr Penfold found we had been paying too much, so we had a rebate going back several years.

Harry Jennings had now left us to work for George Markham, who gave him the use of a pleasant cottage in Stratton Audley, so my father decided to give up the milk deliveries to RAF Bicester which had got us established in dairying.

We had bought a milk float - a small cart which could be pulled by a strong pony - from a local farmer. He had saved his son from having to serve in the First World War by giving him the farm, because whoever was officially the farmer was exempt from call-up. Unfortunately, his son had died towards the end of the war and his widow had sold the farm and cleared off with the proceeds. The old man was left destitute. I had been asking my father to form a partnership with me, but I think that because of what had happened to that poor old farmer, he was reluctant to do it. Although how he could have imagined Daphne could have been capable of such a thing is beyond me – she was such a kindly soul and would never have done anybody a bad turn.

This didn't seem right, as over the years I had put a great deal into the farm including a lot of my money. I had bought a drill, a Vicon rake and an elevator. The drill was £110 and the elevator was about £150. We couldn't have kept going without that equipment.

In 1959 Mr Penfold managed to persuade my father that he should take me into partnership with him. He explained that it would enable him to take a back seat while continuing to take a decent income from the farm. This seemed to satisfy my father. It also marked the start of a new phase in our farming activities which would widen our horizons well beyond Lords Farm.

We had a sad end to the decade however, because in 1959 my dear mother died. She had always been wonderful on the farm and had taken a very active part in calving, poultry and egg production. She made a big contribution to our standard of living with sales of her butter, eggs and poultry, particularly geese and turkeys at Christmas. She used to kill the first goose for Sunday lunch around Michaelmas day, about September 29, and then we would have goose every three weeks or so until they were all gone, except for the birds we kept back for breeding.

Chapter 16

Acquisition and expansion
The 1960s and after

In 1960 we rented as sitting tenants another farm, Rowles Farm at Weston-on-the-Green, which had been farmed by my father's cousin Jack Malins, who had retired. Later, a few years after Jack's death, I was glad to take the opportunity to buy the farm, as land was then hard to come by.

Rowles Farm was heavy land, vastly different from the stone brash of Bicester. When you ploughed it you would turn up great slabs of nasty sticky clay which dried as hard as brick. It took hard winter frost to break it down into a friable tilth which would provide a reasonable seed bed.

The farm was seven miles away, which meant a good deal of travelling, but our little Ferguson tractor could do 20 miles an hour and managed the journey quite quickly. Its twin-furrow plough could deal easily with the land, as long as you tackled it at the right time.

The new rotation we were using to maintain fertility was to plant cocksfoot grass and clover for one, two or three years, then plough the ley up for wheat. After we'd harvested the wheat we would plant kale, then the kale would be ploughed up and we would plant with spring barley, sown under with cocksfoot and clover once again.

My concerns about leaving the RAF early were now easing. By the 1960s it was clear that with care and hard work a living could still be made even from our thin and hungry limestone brash. The manure produced by our dairy herd was beginning to improve the quality and fertility of the soils, and our cereal yields were gradually improving too, giving us a little more profit each year.

In the late 1950s our landlord at Rowles Farm decided it was time to put in a mains water supply. He was a fairly wealthy man, and he decided to lay a pipeline from the mains on the Bicester-Oxford road to the farm. The pipeline would have to cross our land, so he offered to let us take a metered supply for ourselves.

That gave us water at Weston, but we were left with the problem of getting a supply to the various fields we had acquired at Bicester. Many of them would go short of water in dry summers, because the streams would dry up. Lambourne's Ground, about 600 yards from the buildings at Lords Farm, would often go as dry as a bone.

In 1931, to allow the cows at Hill Ground access to water, Harry Jennings and I had dug a waterhole beside the brook there. We dug out a depression which would fill with water, then graded the ground to allow the cattle to get down to it and back. We used a horse-drawn wooden sledge to spread the spoil across the field. To fence our new cattle-drink in, Harry cut down four four-inch willow stakes and drove them into the earth with a sledgehammer. I remember him saying the stakes would take root and grow, and that's exactly what happened. Today they are large willow trees.

That same summer, I can remember helping Harry to put in an oak gatepost at Lords Farm so that we could hang a gate for the orchard. My father suggested we should char the bottom three feet of the wood to prevent it from rotting, so we burned the bottom end of the stake until the outer half inch was charred all the way round. My father was right, because today, nearly 80 years later, that gatepost is still in position.

Talking of these posts reminds me of a poem we learned at school :

> *I remember, I remember the roses red and white,*
> *The violets and the lily cups, those flowers made of light!*
> *The lilacs where the robin built, and where my brother set*
> *The laburnum on his birthday, the tree is living yet!*

Chapter 16

In 1963 our water problem in Bicester was solved in an unexpected way. In 1940 the Air Ministry had sunk a 120-foot bore hole in the field at Lords Farm known as the Little Slade. They wanted to increase the supply of water to RAF Bicester, as demand there was rapidly increasing. Although it produced a flow of 10,000 gallons an hour, the Air Ministry decided this was not enough for their needs, and decided to take the water they needed from the River Cherwell at Lower Heyford.

In the event the council removed the four-inch water main from the borehole to use in extending the mains water supply in the town, and gave us a two-inch replacement. We were able to take a one-inch galvanised pipe from the borehole system as far as Lambourne Ground. Eddie Pickett, who had joined the staff at the farm as a lad of 16, took on the job of laying the pipe, while I played the role of plumber's mate. Having laid the pipe across the bottom of Stepsills field and the brook into Hill Ground, we took it all the way to Lambourne Ground. We took another pipe along the hedge between Stepsills and Stonepits field up into Caversfield Ground.

I engaged a local builder, who had a new Australian hydraulic digger, to install polythene piping across Caversfield Ground to the Long Slade. We decided to leave it under pressure over the weekend before attempting to backfill the trench. That weekend a friend of ours exercising her dog in the field noticed a fine spray and saw that our pipe was leaking. There was a pinhole leak in it and it had ballooned to twice its diameter. Just as well we had decided to leave the pipeline open for inspection, otherwise the leak might not have been discovered for months, even years. Our supplier was only too pleased to replace the pipe with one which was guaranteed to stand the pressure.

All our land could now be grazed in dry summers. We could also grow grass laced with clover in any of our fields, knowing that at any time in summer, autumn or winter the cattle grazing those fields would have access to a clean supply of water. It was a great relief to me to get this done, as the ponds we had relied on in the early days could transmit a variety of diseases, such as bovine TB, to cattle. They were never as clean as they looked. We were now able to fence them off. I'm proud to say that in fact we have never had a case of TB diagnosed in all the years we have been farming around Bicester, although back in the 1930s 40 per cent of all the cattle in the UK were infected.

With all the land we now had we occasionally found ourselves with more grass than we needed, particularly in late autumn. In 1954 or '55 I bought 80 Scotch half-bred ewes to graze the surplus. These animals had been bred in Scotland and were brought down in their thousands to the Midlands and South of England, where they were mated with other breeds, Suffolks or Hampshire Downs.

I bought them as an experiment, but I'm pleased to say they doubled in value in 12 months. My brother-in-law, Eddie Dickins, did the shearing and my father-in-law dipped them along with his own sheep, so the cost of keeping them was very low and they turned in a big profit.

One reason these animals thrived so well was that we'd had no sheep on the farm (except for the lambs we bought in 1945) since my father had sold all his flock during the depression more than 20 years earlier. It's an old and true saying that the sheep's worst enemy is another sheep. Pasture that's been grazed too long without a break becomes 'sheep sick' and worm infestation builds up. The old shepherds used to say that a sheep should not be left to hear the church bells more than three times in the same field. Modern medicines now make worms fairly easy to control, but in those days you had to keep moving them to fresh ground.

Early in the 1960s Richard Collett came to see me once again. This time he told me he was thinking of retiring completely. He had no sons, and his son-in-law, Tom Ward, had died of a heart attack, so he was going to put it on the market, and hoped we would be able to buy it. My father and I decided to do our best to do so.

Chapter 16

The 18th Century five-bedroom farmhouse at Hawkwell and the two pretty cottages still had no electricity or mains water. The farmhouse needed a good deal of renovation and the main barn and stables, which were thatched, needed reroofing. All this, along with the falling profits from agriculture, meant that there was very little competition from other buyers. I went to see the manager of the Midland Bank and told him of our plans and asked for his support, which he gave.

The sale took place at the King's Arms in Bicester on October 10 1962. I told my father that he should be prepared to bid up to £25,000 for the farm, but in the event we got 110 acres, the farmhouse and the cottages for £18,000. This was a great relief to me and to the family, particularly as it meant we now had two charming farm cottages for our workers, so we should no longer find it difficult to recruit.

With the help of Eddie Pickett and his digger we extended our water supply to Hawkwell, and within a few weeks we had arranged for Southern Electricity to connect us to the grid. It would be another 30 years before we would use a little pumping station which had been derequisitioned by the Air Ministry in 1951 to exploit the water supply from the main 15-inch bore. That gave us a supply of water which was at least as clear and pure as our supply from the Cherwell – it had after all been filtered through a hundred feet of limestone. But it did carry a fair amount of lime, which would show up in our kettles and saucepans.

In 1964 Daphne and I moved into Hawkwell Farm. That enabled me to sell the bungalow to Nellie, providing more capital for the business. Nellie much enjoyed living on the farm, and in fact she stayed in the bungalow until she died a few years later, after which my daughter Jenny and her husband moved in.

The next step was to build a milking parlour to enable us to make the most of our much-increased acreage of grazing. To justify the expense we realised we would have to increase the number of cows to around 200, which meant we would also need more accommodation for them. It was a big step forward.

From 1964 Daphne looked after the calf rearing. In the first year she reared over a hundred calves, mostly dairy animals, without loss. We did the same the following year, though we did have some trouble with mucosal disease, which fortunately was treatable. The ringworm which had been a problem at Lords Farm seemed to disappear with our move to Hawkwell and my wife's management.

Raising all those calves successfully was a tremendous achievement for Daphne. Our fortunes were now on a sound footing, with most of our borrowings well covered with the value of our livestock.

In addition to raising calves, running the house and looking after the children and getting them off to school or college, Daphne cared for our poultry. Like my mother she proved to have a great talent for producing laying hens, geese and turkeys for the Christmas trade.

Like the Prince of Wales, who talks to his plants, my wife used to talk to her laying hens. Each hen carried a ring on its leg to indicate the year of its birth, and she knew them all.

I had been concerned that my father should be doing something to reduce his inheritance tax, and suggested he should give me some of his assets to escape death duty, but he was reluctant. I told him: "If you don't think you can trust me, give it straight to your grandsons". And that's what he did. He gave Lords Farm to my sons Tim and John. When he died in January 1969, we had large death duties on the estate, yet I had to pay out my sisters.

Joan inherited the houses in London, and thank goodness she did, because it enabled her to continue caring for Aunt Dora, my father's sister, who had been living with my father since the early 1960s and continued to do so until she died. It was quite a job to sort everything out. I did as much of it as I could myself to avoid paying professional fees.

A few years after we bought Rowles Farm we had an approach from a land agent acting for Prudential Insurance, representing the owners of the Bletchingdon estate. He told me they wanted to buy the whole of the original estate, which had included Rowles Farm, back for the new owners. They wanted 110 acres of land there and made a surprisingly high offer for it, considering that it was heavy land and not as easy to manage as our land at Bicester and with only a small cottage and few buildings.

I accepted, rather reluctantly. However, it turned out to be a good move. It enabled me to buy Wharf Farm at Souldern, which had 70 acres of land plus an attractive farmhouse by the canal and a chalet bungalow which had been built only ten years before by a rich antique dealer whose son was keen to be a farmer. When the son got tired of having to work seven days a week and gave up farming, it went back on the market.

The land at Wharf Farm was on the flood plain of the river Cherwell and up to 40 acres of it could be flooded if we had heavy rain, but there was plenty of good grazing above the flood level.

My son John took on the farmhouse and brought the buildings up to date. He built new loose boxes for calving cows and their calves, and improved the milking parlour, which meant that we could start milking there as well as at Hawkwell. John and his family have lived happily at Souldern ever since.

Having established a larger milking herd at Hawkwell and set up another herd at Wharf Farm, we felt we were at last in a position to reap the rewards of all our hard work and expense - as long as milk production remained profitable. Unfortunately we now saw the beginning of a steady fall in milk prices which was to continue for the next 20 years. Dairying became less and less attractive, and many decent farmers packed it in.

With our meagre profits, helped by borrowing from the bank when we had to, we were still able to buy suitable land when it became available. We bought 120 acres between Somerton and Fritwell (near Souldern) at about £3000 an acre, a great risk as the outlook at that time was not favourable. This land was slightly deeper and richer loam and would yield at least a quarter of a ton of wheat per acre more than our thinner land at Hawkwell. By the end of the century we had also acquired ten acres from the sale of Aldershot Farm and a further 50 acres next to it.

The years of living dangerously might have seemed long over, but fate still had one or two close shaves in store for me. One hot summer's afternoon in the mid 1970s while the men were haymaking, Daphne and I went over to Stonepits Fields, where the milking herd was grazing. We opened the gate to let the cattle into Home Ground on their way to the dairy, and I told Daphne to stand in the angle of the gate and the hedge, where she would be out of the way of the cattle as they passed through.

As I called up the herd, the cows started getting up and walking towards the gate. A few cows were still lying down with the Friesian bull, so I got them up and kicked the bull on the nose. He got up and took a couple of paces backwards, and the next thing I knew he smacked into me with a great wallop in the lower part of the chest. I went up in the air and fell down on to my back.

The bull came in again and rolled his head over my thigh. I grabbed his head chain and he backed away, pulling the chain from my hand. I was afraid he would come in again, but the disturbance, and the sight of me on the ground, had been enough to bring most of the cows back to form a rough circle around me, and I was able to get to my feet. It was almost as if the cows were defending me.

I shouted to Daphne to stand behind the gate and quietly drove the herd out of the field with the bull following them. I suffered nothing more serious than a slightly bruised chest, but my shoulders and the top of my back bore a delightful imprint of the Aertex vest I was wearing. We sent the bull away for slaughter two or three days later.

Then, in the summer of 1984, I had to drive to Frogleys Farm to do some tedding (turning over hay to help it to dry). I had just picked up a brand new Austin Princess, and was still getting used to it. The route took me over an unmanned crossing on the Oxford-Bletchley railway line, which carried about four trains a day.

As I approached the railway line I stopped to listen for a train, but all seemed silent, so I started to move forward. My vision to the right had been obscured by a hedge. As I crossed the view opened up - and I looked along the track to see a train bearing down on me at a terrifying speed.

I think I must have tried to put the car into reverse, but selected a forward gear by mistake. The train hit the car full on, and the left buffer came straight through my open window. The Austin and I travelled some 150 yards down the track before the train finally came to a halt. The car had begun to disintegrate, and the gearbox had fallen on to the track.

Somehow it seems I managed to open the door and walk back towards the crossing, although I can remember nothing about it. Some people in a small factory beside the crossing heard the crash and came to my aid. They took me into their offices and bathed my head, which was bleeding heavily. Within ten minutes an ambulance had arrived, and I was taken to the old Radcliffe Infirmary in Oxford.

I remember telling the attractive young ambulance girl, in a lucid moment, that during the war my job had involved attacking trains in France and Belgium and that now the trains had got their own back. By some miracle I had escaped serious injury, but they kept me in hospital for a couple of days under observation.

Some weeks later I had to report to a senior member of the British Transport Police in Oxford, where I was suitably admonished and warned to drive more carefully in future. They handed me back the possessions I had left in the car, which included a whisky bottle containing lemonade and a copy of Private Eye. I remember asking the policeman if he enjoyed reading the Eye, and he said "Oh no, I never read stuff like that". I think he imagined it was pornography.

Chapter 16

Over the years the outlook for farming slowly improved. In 2007 milk prices suddenly increased substantially, which at last restored confidence in milk production. A shortage of milk in the UK would have forced us to import milk from the continent, when we would have been at the mercy of European producers and suffered all the expense of transporting milk in refrigerated lorries from France or Holland.

Corn prices went up at about the same time, so we were finally able to reap the rewards of all our investment in land.

By the end of the 20th Century we were at last providing a fair living for myself and my sons. This achievement pleased Daphne greatly, since she had played such a huge part in making it possible. She said she had never imagined that one day she would be in a partnership which owned more than 500 acres of land.

Her father had been a first-rate farmer himself, but he was a tenant who had had to move from one farm to another. When he died at 71 his last tenancy had ended, so that was the end of farming for the Dickins family. I'm sure Daphne's father would have been delighted to see how successful she became after his lifetime.

I owe a lot to Daphne. It was a great sadness when she died in December 2008.

Postscript

It is now more than a century since my grandfather bought Lords Farm in 1901. Back in the 1920s we had three men to farm 100 acres. Today we still only employ three men, but we farm 900 acres. Advances in machinery since the 1920s have clearly helped us a great deal.

We have come a long way. If I could go back in time, would I change anything? I don't think I would.

I write these last words at the start of my 96th year. You may ask - what have I have achieved? Did I do the right thing in throwing up a successful career in the RAF and coming back to keep the farm going?

Today, with land prices averaging £6000 an acre and farmhouses vastly increased in value, the modest farming enterprise started by my grandfather has grown into a business with assets worth several million pounds. The 900 acres of land I farm with my sons has been designated the site of the first Eco Town in England. Not a bad return for a lifetime which has been so rewarding and enjoyable.

We could not have achieved all this without with the help of our loyal staff, including the very capable David Spencer, who manages the arable side of the business and has given more than 30 years' service to the farm. Many good friends have also assisted us at busy times, in particular George Davies. I must not forget to mention my granddaughter Holly, who has worked until three in the morning stacking big bales with the JCB teleloader in order to avoid the rain.

I am too old and feeble now to go on enjoying to any great extent the fruits of my labours, but at least I have the satisfaction of knowing that I have done my best to ensure that my descendants have a slightly easier life than the one I had.

It is only necessary now for my sons and grandson to take up the challenge and continue farming steadily in the same way to ensure that the business continues to be successful and to provide a decent living for those members of the family who are prepared to shoulder the burden of farming this hungry land.

In thinking about all this I am reminded of a slip of paper I found in my mother's prayer book many years ago, when I borrowed it one Sunday to take to church. She had written her favourite prayer inside it. The lines I remember best from it are these:

"O Lord support us all the day long of this troublous life, until the shadows lengthen and the evening comes, the busy world is hushed, the fever of life is over and our work is done. Then Lord, in thy mercy, grant us safe lodging, a holy rest and peace at the last."

THE END

Proof

Made in the USA
Charleston, SC
19 January 2011